☑ S0-BEI-484

Pass the COMPASS!

COMPASS® Study Guide and Practice Test Questions

Published by

Complete TEST
Preparation Inc.

We strongly recommend that students check with exam providers for up-to-date information regarding test content.

ISBN-13: 978-1928077329 (Complete Test Preparation Inc.)
ISBN-10: 1928077323

Version 6 August 2014

Published by
Complete Test Preparation Inc.
921 Foul Bay Rd.
Victoria BC Canada V8S 4H9
Visit us on the web at http://www.test-preparation.ca
Printed in the USA

About Complete Test Preparation

The Complete Test Preparation Team has been publishing high quality study materials since 2005. Thousands of students visit our websites every year, and thousands of students, teachers and parents all over the world have purchased our teaching materials, curriculum, study guides and practice tests.

Complete Test Preparation is committed to providing students with the best study materials and practice tests available on the market. Members of our team combine years of teaching experience, with experienced writers and editors, all with advanced degrees.

Team Members for this publication

Editor: Brian Stocker MA
Contributor: Dr. C. Gregory
Contributor: Dr. G. A. Stocker DDS
Contributor: D. A. Stocker M. Ed.
Contributor: Sheila M. Hynes, MES York, BA (Hons)
Contributor: Elizabeta Petrovic MSc (Mathematics)
Contributor: Kelley O'Malley BA (English)

Feedback

We welcome your feedback. Email us at feedback@test-preparation.ca with your comments and suggestions. We carefully review all suggestions and often incorporate reader suggestions into upcoming versions. As a Print on Demand Publisher, we update our products frequently.

 ## Find us on Facebook

www.facebook.com/CompleteTestPreparation

The Environment and Sustainability

Environmental consciousness is important for the continued growth of our company. Besides eco-balancing each title, as a print on demand publisher, we only print units as orders come in, which greatly reduces excess printing and waste. This revolutionary printing technology also eliminates carbon emissions from trucks hauling boxes of books everywhere to warehouses. We also maintain a commitment to recycling any waste materials that may result from the printing process. We continue to review our manufacturing practices on an ongoing basis to ensure we are doing our part to protect and improve the environment.

Contents

Getting Started

CONGRATULATIONS! By deciding to take the COMPASS® Exam, you have taken the first step toward a great future! Of course, there is no point in taking this important examination unless you intend to do your very best in order to earn the highest grade you possibly can. That means getting yourself organized and discovering the best approaches, methods and strategies to master the material. Yes, that will require real effort and dedication on your part but if you are willing to focus your energy and devote the study time necessary, before you know it you will be on you will be opening that letter of acceptance to the school of your dreams!

We know that taking on a new endeavour can be a little scary, and it is easy to feel unsure of where to begin. That's where we come in. This study guide is designed to help you improve your test-taking skills, show you a few tricks of the trade and increase both your competency and confidence.

The COMPASS Exam

The COMPASS® exam is composed of four main sections, reading, mathematics, writing skills and writing. The reading section consists of reading comprehension questions. The mathematics section contains, arithmetic, algebra, geometry and polynomials, quadratic equations, quadrilaterals, trigonometry, logarithms and sequences. The writing skills section contains questions on sentence structure and rewriting sentences. The writing section contains an essay question.

The COMPASS exam is computer based and adaptive. This means if you answer a questions correctly, the next question will be more difficulty until you reach your level of difficulty. If you answer incorrectly and you are not already at the lowest level of difficulty, the next question will be easier. Each question is multiple-choice, and the exact number of questions varies from student to student depending on how skilled the student is in a particular area.

While we seek to make our guide as comprehensive as possible, note that like all exams, the COMPASS® Exam might be adjusted at some future point. New material might be added, or content that is no longer relevant or applicable might be removed. It is always a good idea to give the materials you receive when you register to take the COMPASS® a careful review.

How this study guide is organized

This study guide is divided into four sections. The first section, Self-Assessments, which will help you recognize your areas of strength and weaknesses. This will be a boon when it comes to managing your study time most efficiently; there is not much point of focusing on material you have already got firmly under control. Instead, taking the self-assessments will show you where that time could be much better spent. In this area you will begin with a few questions to quickly evaluate your understanding of material that is likely to appear on the COMPASS®. If you do poorly in certain areas, simply work carefully through those sections in the tutorials and then try the self-assessment again.

The second section, Tutorials, offers information in each of the content areas, as well as strategies to help you master that material. The tutorials are not intended to be a complete course, but cover general principals. If you find that you do not understand the tutorials, it is recommended that you seek out additional instruction.

Third, we offer two sets of practice test questions, similar to those on the COMPASS® Exam.

The COMPASS® Study Plan

Now that you have made the decision to take the COM-PASS®, it is time to get started. Before you do another thing, you will need to figure out a plan of attack. The very best study tip is to start early! The longer the time period you devote to regular study practice, the more likely you will be to retain the material and be able to access it quickly. If you thought that 1x20 is the same as 2x10, guess what? It really is not, when it comes to study time. Reviewing material for just an hour per day over the course of 20 days is far better than studying for two hours a day for only 10 days. The more often you revisit a particular piece of information, the better you will know it. Not only will your grasp and understanding be better, but your ability to reach into your brain and quickly and efficiently pull out the tidbit you need, will be greatly enhanced as well.

The great Chinese scholar and philosopher Confucius believed that true knowledge could be defined as knowing both what you know and what you do not know. The first step in preparing for the COMPASS® is to assess your strengths and weaknesses. You may already have an idea of what you know and what you do not know, but evaluating yourself using our Self- Assessment modules for each of the three areas, Math, Writing and Reading Comprehension, will clarify the details.

Making a Study Schedule

In order to make your study time most productive you will need to develop a study plan. The purpose of the plan is to organize all the bits of pieces of information in such a way that you will not feel overwhelmed. Rome was not built in a day, and learning everything you will need to know in order to pass the COMPASS® is going to take time, too. Arranging the material you need to learn into manageable chunks is the best way to go. Each study session should make you feel as though you have succeeded in accomplishing your goal, and your goal is simply to learn what you planned to learn during that particular session. Try to organize the content in such a way that each study session builds on previous ones. That way, you will retain the information, be better able to access it, and review the previous bits and pieces at the same time.

Self-assessment

The Best Study Tip! The very best study tip is to start early! The longer you study regularly, the more you will retain and 'learn' the material. Studying for 1 hour per day for 20 days is far better than studying for 2 hours for 10 days.

What don't you know?

The first step is to assess your strengths and weaknesses. You may already have an idea of where your weaknesses are, or you can take our Self-assessment modules for each of the areas, Reading Comprehension, Arithmetic, Essay Writing, Algebra and College Level Math.

Exam Component	Rate 1 to 5
Reading Comprehension	
Making Inferences	
Main idea	
Arithmetic	
Decimals Percent and Fractions	
Problem solving (Word Problems)	
Basic Algebra	
Simple Geometry	
Problem Solving	

Essay Writing	
Writing skills	
Sentence Correction	
Basic English Grammar and Usage	
Algebra	
Exponents	
Linear Equations	
Quadratics	
Polynomials	
College Level	
Coordinate Geometry	
Trigonometry	
Polynomials	
Logarithms	
Sequences	

Making a Study Schedule

The key to making a study plan is to divide the material you need to learn into manageable size and learn it, while at the same time reviewing the material that you already know.

Using the table above, any scores of three or below, you need to spend time learning, going over, and practicing this subject area. A score of four means you need to review the material, but you don't have to spend time re-learning. A score of five and you are OK with just an occasional review before the exam.

A score of zero or one means you really do need to work on this and you should allocate the most time and give it the highest priority. Some students prefer a 5-day plan and oth-

ers a 10-day plan.   It also depends on how much time you
have until the exam.

Here is an example of a 5-day plan based on an example
from the table above:

Main Idea: 1   Study 1 hour everyday – review on last day
Fractions: 3   Study 1 hour for 2 days then ½ hour and
then review
Algebra: 4   Review every second day
Grammar & Usage: 2 Study 1 hour on the first day – then ½
hour everyday
Reading Comprehension: 5   Review for ½ hour every
other day
Geometry: 5 Review for ½ hour every other day

Using this example, geometry and reading comprehension are good and only need occasional review.   Algebra is
good and needs 'some' review. Fractions need a bit of work,
grammar and usage needs a lot of work and Main Idea is
very weak and need most of time.   Based on this, here is a
sample study plan:

Day	Subject	Time
Monday		
Study	Main Idea	1 hour
Study	Grammar & Usage	1 hour
	½ hour break	
Study	Fractions	1 hour
Review	Algebra	½ hour
Tuesday		
Study	Main Idea	1 hour
Study	Grammar & Usage	½ hour
	½ hour break	
Study	Fractions	½ hour
Review	Algebra	½ hour
Review	Geometry	½ hour
Wednesday		
Study	Main Idea	1 hour

Study	Grammar & Usage	½ hour
	½ hour break	
Study	Fractions	½ hour
Review	Geometry	½ hour
Thursday		
Study	Main Idea	½ hour
Study	Grammar & Usage	½ hour
Review	Fractions	½ hour
	½ hour break	
Review	Geometry	½ hour
Review	Algebra	½ hour
Friday		
Review	Main Idea	½ hour
Review	Grammar & Usage	½ hour
Review	Fractions	½ hour
	½ hour break	
Review	Algebra	½ hour
Review	Grammar & Usage	½ hour

Using this example, adapt the study plan to your own schedule. This schedule assumes 2 ½ - 3 hours available to study everyday for a 5 day period.

First, write out what you need to study and how much. Next figure out how many days you have before the test. Note, do NOT study on the last day before the test. On the last day before the test, you won't learn anything and will probably only confuse yourself.

Make a table with the days before the test and the number of hours you have available to study each day. We suggest working with 1 hour and ½ hour time slots.

Start filling in the blanks, with the subjects you need to study the most getting the most time and the most regular time slots (i.e. everyday) and the subjects that you know getting the least time (e.g. ½ hour every other day, or every 3rd day).

Tips for making a schedule

Once you make a schedule, stick with it! Make your study sessions reasonable. If you make a study schedule and don't stick with it, you set yourself up for failure. Instead, schedule study sessions that are a bit shorter and set yourself up for success! Make sure your study sessions are do-able. Studying is hard work but after you pass, you can party and take a break!

Schedule breaks. Breaks are just as important as study time. Work out a rotation of studying and breaks that works for you.

Build up study time. If you find it hard to sit still and study for 1 hour straight through, build up to it. Start with 20 minutes, and then take a break. Once you get used to 20-minute study sessions, increase the time to 30 minutes. Gradually work you way up to 1 hour.

40 minutes to 1 hour are optimal. Studying for longer than this is tiring and not productive. Studying for shorter isn't long enough to be productive.

Studying Math. Studying Math is different from studying other subjects because you use a different part of your brain. The best way to study math is to practice everyday. This will train your mind to think in a mathematical way. If you miss a day or days, the mathematical mind-set is gone and you have to start all over again to build it up.

Study and practice math everyday for at least 5 days before the exam.

Reading Comprehension

THIS SECTION CONTAINS A SELF-ASSESSMENT AND READING TUTO-
RIAL. The tutorials are designed to familiarize general
principals and the self-assessment contains general
questions similar to the reading questions likely to be on the
COMPASS®, but are not intended to be identical to the exam
questions. The tutorials are not designed to be a complete
reading course, and it is assumed that students have some
familiarity with reading comprehension questions. If you do
not understand parts of the tutorial, or find the tutorial difficult, it is recommended that you seek out additional instruction.

Tour of the COMPASS Reading Comprehension Content

Below is a more detailed list of the types of reading comprehension questions that generally appear on the COMPASS®.
Make sure you understand all of these points at a very minimum.

- Draw logical conclusions

- Identify the main idea

- Identify secondary ideas

- Identify the author's intent

The questions below are not the same as you will find on
the COMPASS® - that would be too easy! And nobody knows
what the questions will be and they change all the time.
Mostly the changes consist of substituting new questions for
old, but the changes can be new question formats or styles,
changes to the number of questions in each section, changes
to the time limits for each section and combining sections.
Below are general reading questions that cover the same areas as the COMPASS®. While the format and exact wording
of the questions may differ slightly, and change from year to

year, if you can answer the questions below, you will have no problem with the reading section of the COMPASS®.

Reading Comprehension Self-Assessment

The purpose of the self-assessment is:

- Identify your strengths and weaknesses.

- Develop your personalized study plan (above)

- Get accustomed to the COMPASS® format

- Extra practice – the self-assessments are almost a full 3rd practice test!

- Provide a baseline score for preparing your study schedule.

Since this is a Self-assessment, and depending on how confident you are with Reading Comprehension, timing is optional. A general rule is one minute per question, so allow 25 minutes to complete this self-assessment. Once complete, use the table below to assess your understanding of the content, and prepare your study schedule described in chapter 1.

80% - 100%	Excellent – you have mastered the content
60 – 79%	Good. You have a working knowledge. Even though you can just pass this section, you may want to review the tutorials and do some extra practice to see if you can improve your mark.

| 40% - 59% | Below Average. You do not understand the reading comprehension problems. Review the tutorials , and retake this quiz again in a few days, before proceeding to the practice test questions. |
| Less than 40% | Poor. You have a very limited understanding of the reading comprehension problems.

Please review the tutorials , and retake this quiz again in a few days, before proceeding to the practice test questions. |

Reading Self-Assessment Answer Sheet

1. (A) (B) (C) (D) 11. (A) (B) (C) (D) 21. (A) (B) (C) (D)

2. (A) (B) (C) (D) 12. (A) (B) (C) (D) 22. (A) (B) (C) (D)

3. (A) (B) (C) (D) 13. (A) (B) (C) (D) 23. (A) (B) (C) (D)

4. (A) (B) (C) (D) 14. (A) (B) (C) (D) 24. (A) (B) (C) (D)

5. (A) (B) (C) (D) 15. (A) (B) (C) (D) 25. (A) (B) (C) (D)

6. (A) (B) (C) (D) 16. (A) (B) (C) (D)

7. (A) (B) (C) (D) 17. (A) (B) (C) (D)

8. (A) (B) (C) (D) 18. (A) (B) (C) (D)

9. (A) (B) (C) (D) 19. (A) (B) (C) (D)

10. (A) (B) (C) (D) 20. (A) (B) (C) (D)

Questions 1 – 4 refer to the following passage.

Passage 1 - The Immune System

An immune system is a system of biological structures and processes that protects against disease by identifying and killing pathogens and other threats. The immune system can detect a wide variety of agents, from viruses to parasitic worms, and distinguish them from the organism's own healthy cells and tissues. Detection is complicated as pathogens evolve rapidly to avoid the immune system defences, and successfully infect their hosts.

The human immune system consists of many types of proteins, cells, organs, and tissues, which interact in an elaborate and dynamic network. As part of this more complex immune response, the human immune system adapts over time to recognize specific pathogens more efficiently. This adaptation process is called "adaptive immunity" or "acquired immunity" and creates immunological memory. Immunological memory created from a primary response to a specific pathogen, provides an enhanced response to future encounters with that same pathogen. This process of acquired immunity is the basis of vaccination. [1]

1. What can we infer from the first paragraph in this passage?

    a. When a person's body fights off the flu, this is the immune system in action

    b. When a person's immune system functions correctly, they avoid all sicknesses and injuries

    c. When a person's immune system is weak, a person will likely get a terminal disease

    d. When a person's body fights off a cold, this is the circulatory system in action

2. The immune system's primary function is to:

a. Strengthen the bones

b. Protect against disease

c. Improve respiration

d. Improve circulation

3. Based on the passage, what can we say about evolution's role in the immune system?

a. Evolution of the immune system is an important factor in the immune system's efficiency

b. Evolution causes a person to die, thus killing the pathogen

c. Evolution plays no known role in immunity

d. The least evolved earth species have better immunity

4. Which sentence below, taken from the passage, tell us the main idea of the passage?

a. The human immune system consists of many types of proteins, cells, organs, and tissues, which interact in an elaborate and dynamic network.

b. An immune system is a system of biological structures and processes that protects against disease by identifying and killing pathogens and other threats.

c. The immune system can detect a wide variety of agents, from viruses to parasitic worms, and distinguish them from the organism's own healthy cells and tissues.

d. None of these express the main idea.

Questions 5 – 8 refer to the following passage.

Passage 2 - White Blood Cells

White blood cells (WBCs), or leukocytes (also spelled "leucocytes"), are cells of the immune system that defend the body against both infectious disease and foreign material. Five different and diverse types of leukocytes exist, but they are all produced and derived from a powerful cell in the bone marrow known as a hematopoietic stem cell. Leukocytes are found throughout the body, including the blood and lymphatic system.

The number of WBCs in the blood is often an indicator of disease. There are normally between 4×10^9 and 1.1×10^{10} white blood cells in a liter of blood, making up about 1% of blood in a healthy adult. The physical properties of white blood cells, such as volume, conductivity, and granularity, changes due to the presence of immature cells, or malignant cells.

The name white blood cell derives from the fact that after processing a blood sample in a centrifuge, the white cells are typically a thin, white layer of nucleated cells. The scientific term leukocyte directly reflects this description, derived from Greek leukos (white), and kytos (cell). [2]

5. What can we infer from the first paragraph in this selection?

a. Red blood cells are not as important as white blood cells

b. White blood cells are the culprits in most infectious diseases

c. White blood cells are essential to fight off infectious diseases

d. Red blood cells are essential to fight off infectious diseases

6. What can we say about the number of white blood cells in a liter of blood?

a. They make up about 1% of a healthy adult's blood

b. There are 10^{10} WBCs in a healthy adult's blood

c. The number varies according to age

d. They are a thin white layer of nucleated cells

7. What is a more scientific term for "white blood cell"?

a. Red blood cell

b. Anthrocyte

c. Leukocyte

d. Leukemia

8. Can the number of leukocytes indicate cancer?

a. Yes, the white blood cell count can indicate disease.

b. No, the white blood cell count is not a reliable indicator.

c. Disease may indicate a high white blood cell count.

d. None of the choices are correct.

Questions 9 – 12 refer to the following passage.

Keeping Tropical Fish

Keeping tropical fishe at home or in your office used to be very popular. Today, interest has declined, but it remains as rewarding and relaxing a hobby as ever. Ask any tropical fish hobbyist, and you will hear how soothing and relaxing watching colorful fish live their lives in the aquarium. If you are considering keeping tropical fish as pets, here is a list of the basic equipment you will need.

A filter is essential for keeping your aquarium clean and your fish alive and healthy. There are different types and sizes of filters and the right size for you depends on the size of the aquarium and the level of stocking. Generally, you need a filter with a 3 to 5 times turn over rate per hour. This means that the water in the tank should go through the filter about 3 to 5 times per hour.

Most tropical fish do well in water temperatures ranging between 24° C and 26° C, though each has its own ideal water temperature. A heater with a thermostat is necessary to regulate the water temperature. Some heaters are submersible and others are not, so check carefully before you buy.

Lights are also necessary, and come in a large variety of types, strengths and sizes. A light source is necessary for plants in the tank to photosynthesize and give the tank a more attractive appearance. Even if you plan on using plastic plants, the fish still require light, although here you can use a lower strength light source.

A hood is necessary to keep dust, dirt and unwanted materials out of the tank. Sometimes the hood can also help prevent evaporation. Another requirement is aquarium gravel. This will improve the aesthetics of the aquarium and is necessary if you plan on having real plants.

9. What is the general tone of this article?

    a. Formal

    b. Informal

    c. Technical

    d. Opinion

10. Which of the following can not be inferred?

    a. Gravel is good for aquarium plants.

    b. Fewer people have aquariums in their office than at home.

    c. The larger the tank, the larger the filter required.

    d. None of the above.

11. What evidence does the author provide to support their claim that aquarium lights are necessary?

    a. Plants require light.

    b. Fish and plants require light.

    c. The author does not provide evidence for this statement.

    d. Aquarium lights make the aquarium more attractive.

12. Which of the following is an opinion?

    a. Filter with a 3 to 5 times turn over rate per hour are required.

    b. Aquarium gravel improves the aesthetics of the aquarium.

    c. An aquarium hood keeps dust, dirt and unwanted materials out of the tank.

    d. Each type of tropical fish has its own ideal water temperature.

Questions 13 – 14 refer to the following passage.

Vice President Johnson, Mr. Speaker, Mr. Chief Justice, President Eisenhower, Vice President Nixon, President Truman, reverend clergy, fellow citizens:

We observe today not a victory of party, but a celebration of freedom -- symbolizing an end, as well as a beginning -- signifying renewal, as well as change. For I have sworn before you and Almighty God the same solemn oath our forebears prescribed nearly a century and three-quarters ago.

The world is very different now. For man holds in his mortal hands the power to abolish all forms of human poverty and all forms of human life. And yet the same revolutionary beliefs for which our forebears fought are still at issue around the globe -- the belief that the rights of man come not from the generosity of the state, but from the hand of God.

We dare not forget today that we are the heirs of that first revolution. Let the word go forth from this time and place, to friend and foe alike, that the torch has been passed to a new generation of Americans -- born in this century, tempered by war, disciplined by a hard and bitter peace, proud of our ancient heritage, and unwilling to witness or permit the slow undoing of those human rights to which this nation has always been committed, and to which we are committed today at home and around the world.

Let every nation know, whether it wishes us well or ill, that we shall pay any price, bear any burden, meet any hardship, support any friend, oppose any foe, to assure the survival and the success of liberty.

This much we pledge -- and more.

John F. Kennedy Inaugural Address 20 January 1961

13. What is the tone of this speech?

    a. Triumphant

    b. Optimistic

    c. Threatening

    d. Gloating

14. Which of the following is an opinion?

a. The world is very different now.

b. For man holds in his mortal hands the power to abolish all forms of human poverty and all forms of human life.

c. We dare not forget today that we are the heirs of that first revolution

d. For I have sworn before you and Almighty God the same solemn oath our forebears prescribed nearly a century and three-quarters ago.

Questions 15 – 18 refer to the following passage.

If You Have Allergies, You're Not Alone

People who experience allergies might joke that their immune systems have let them down or are seriously lacking. Truthfully though, people who experience allergic reactions or allergy symptoms during certain times of the year have heightened immune systems that are, "better" than those of people who have perfectly healthy but less militant immune systems.

Still, when a person has an allergic reaction, they are having an adverse reaction to a substance that is considered normal to most people. Mild allergic reactions usually have symptoms like itching, runny nose, red eyes, or bumps or discoloration of the skin. More serious allergic reactions, such as those to animal and insect poisons or certain foods, may result in the closing of the throat, swelling of the eyes, low blood pressure, inability to breath, and can even be fatal.

Different treatments help different allergies, and which one a person uses depends on the nature and severity of the allergy. It is recommended to patients with severe allergies to take extra precautions, such as carrying an EpiPen, which treats anaphylactic shock and may prevent death, always in order for the remedy to be readily available and more effective. When an allergy is not so severe, treatments may be used just relieve a person of uncomfortable symptoms. Over the counter allergy medicines treat milder symptoms, and can be bought at any grocery store and used in moderation to help people with allergies live normally.

There are many tests available to assess whether a person has allergies or what they may be allergic to, and advances in these tests and the medicine used to treat patients continues to improve. Despite this fact, allergies still affect a large number of people throughout the year or even every day. Medicines used to treat allergies have side effects of their own, and it is difficult to bring the body into balance with the use of medicine. Regardless, many of those who live with allergies are grateful for what is available and find it useful in maintaining their lifestyles.

15. According to this passage, it can be understood that the word "militant" belongs in a group with the words:

  a. a. sickly, ailing, faint

  b. b. strength, power, vigor

  c. c. active, fighting, warring

  d. d. worn, tired, breaking down

16. The author says that "medicines used to treat allergies have side effects of their own" in order to

  a. point out that doctors aren't very good at diagnosing and treating allergies

  b. argue that because of the large number of people with allergies, a cure will never be found

  c. explain that allergy medicines aren't cures and some compromise must be made

  d. argue that more wholesome remedies should be researched and medicines banned

17. It can be inferred that _____ recommend that some people with allergies carry medicine with them.

  a. the author

  b. doctors

  c. the makers of EpiPen

  d. people with allergies

18. The author has written this passage in order to

  a. inform readers on symptoms of allergies so people with allergies can get help

  b. persuade readers to be proud of having allergies

  c. inform readers on different remedies so people with allergies receive the right help

  d. describe different types of allergies, their symptoms, and their remedies

Questions 19 – 22 refer to the following passage.

When a Poet Longs to Mourn, He Writes an Elegy

Poems are an expressive, especially emotional, form of writing. They have been present in literature virtually from the time civilizations invented the written word. Poets often portrayed as moody, secluded, and even troubled, but this is because poets are introspective and feel deeply about the current events and cultural norms they are surrounded with. Poets often produce the most telling literature, giving insight into the society and mindset they come from. This can be done in many forms.

The oldest types of poems often include many stanzas, may or may not rhyme, and are more about telling a story than experimenting with language or words. The most common types of ancient poetry are epics, which are usually extremely long stories that follow a hero through his journey, or ellegies, which are often solemn in tone and used to mourn or lament something or someone. The Mesopotamians are often said to have invented the written word, and their literature is among the oldest in the world, including the epic poem titled "Epic of Gilgamesh". Similar in style and length to "Gilgamesh" is "Beowulf", an ellegy poem written in Old English and set in Scandinavia. These poems are often used by professors as the earliest examples of literature.

The importance of poetry was revived in the Renaissance. At this time, Europeans discovered the style and beauty of ancient Greek arts, and poetry was among those. Shakespeare is the most well-known poet of the time, and he used poetry not only to write poems but also to write plays for the theater. The most popular forms of poetry during the Renaissance included villanelles, sonnets, as well as the epic. Poets during this time focused on style and form, and developed very specific rules and outlines for how an exceptional poem should be written.

As often happens in the arts, modern poets have rejected the constricting rules of Renaissance poets, and free form poems are much more popular. Some modern poems would read just like stories if they weren't arranged into lines and stanzas. It is difficult to tell which poems and poets will be the most important, because works of art often become more famous in hindsight, after the poet has died and society can look at itself without being in the moment. Modern poetry continues to develop, and will no doubt continue to change as values, thought, and writing continue to change.

Poems can be among the most enlightening and uplifting texts for a person to read if they are looking to connect with the past, connect with other people, or try to gain an understanding of what is happening in their time.

19. In summary, the author has written this passage

   a. as a foreword that will introduce a poem in a book or magazine

   b. because she loves poetry and wants more people to like it

   c. to give a brief history of poems

   d. in order to convince students to write poems

20. The author organizes the paragraphs mainly by

   a. moving chronologically, explaining which types of poetry were common in that time

   b. talking about new types of poems each paragraph and explaining them a little

   c. focusing on one poet or group of people and the poems they wrote

   d. explaining older types of poetry so she can talk about modern poetry

21. The author's claim that poetry has been around "virtually from the time civilizations invented the written word" is supported by the detail that

a. Beowulf is written in Old English, which is not really in use any longer

b. epic poems told stories about heroes

c. the Renaissance poets tried to copy Greek poets

d. the Mesopotamians are credited with both inventing the word and writing "Epic of Gilgamesh"

22. According to the passage, it can be understood that the word "telling" means

a. speaking

b. significant

c. soothing

d. wordy

Questions 23 – 25 refer to the following passage.

Winged Victory of Samothrace: the Statue of the Gods

Students who read about the "Winged Victory of Samothrace" probably won't be able to picture what this statue looks like. However, almost anyone who knows a little about statues will recognize it when they see it: it is the statue of a winged woman who does not have arms or a head. Even the most famous pieces of art may be recognized by sight but not by name.

This iconic statue is of the Greek goddess Nike, who represented victory and was called Victoria by the Romans. The statue is sometimes called the "Nike of Samothrace". She was often displayed in Greek art as driving a chariot, and her speed or efficiency with the chariot may be what her wings symbolize. It is said that the statue was created around 200 BCE to celebrate a battle that was won at sea. Archaeologists and art historians believe the statue may have originally been part of a temple or other building, even one of the most important temples, Megaloi Theoi, just as many statues were used during that time.

"Winged Victory" does indeed appear to have had arms and a head when it was originally created, and it is unclear why they were removed or lost. Indeed, they have never been discovered, even with all the excavation that has taken place. Many speculate that one of her arms was raised and put to her mouth, as though she was shouting or calling out, which is consistent with the idea of her as a war figure. If the missing pieces were ever to be found, they might give Greek and art historians more of an idea of what Nike represented or how the statue was used.

Learning about pieces of art through details like these can help students remember time frames or locations, as well as learn about the people who occupied them.

23. The author's title says the statue is "of the Gods" because

a. the statue is very beautiful and even a god would find it beautiful

b. the statue is of a Greek goddess, and gods were of primary importance to the Greek

d. Nike lead the gods into war

d. the statues were used at the temple of the gods and so it belonged to them

24. The third paragraph states that

a. the statue is related to war and was probably broken apart by foreign soldiers

b. the arms and head of the statue cannot be found because all the excavation has taken place

c. speculations have been made about what the entire statue looked like and what it symbolized

d. the statue has no arms or head because the sculptor lost them

25. The author's main purpose in writing this passage is to

a. demonstrate that art and culture are related and one can teach us about the other

b. persuade readers to become archeologists and find the missing pieces of the statue

c. teach readers about the Greek goddess Nike

d. to teach readers the name of a statue they probably recognize

Reading Self-Assessment Answer Key

1. A
The passage does not mention the flu specifically, however we know the flu is a pathogen (a bacterium, virus, or other microorganism that can cause disease). Therefore, we can infer, when a person's body fights off the flu, this is the immune system in action.

2. B
The immune system's primary function is to protect against disease.

3. A
The passage refers to evolution of the immune system being important for efficiency. In paragraph three, there is a discussion of adaptive and acquired immunity, where the immune system "remembers" pathogens.

We can determine, evolution of the immune system is an important factor in the immune system's efficiency.

4. B
The sentence that expresses the main idea of the passage is, "An immune system is a system of biological structures and processes that protects against disease by identifying and killing pathogens and other threats."

5. C
We can infer white blood cells are essential to fight off infectious diseases, from the passage, "cells of the immune system that defend the body against both infectious disease and foreign material."

6. A
We can say the number of white blood cells in a liter of blood make up about 1% of a healthy adult's blood. This is a fact-based question that is easy and fast to answer. The question asks about a percentage. You can quickly and easily scan the passage for the percent sign, or the word percent and find the answer.

7. C

A more scientific term for "white blood cell" is leukocyte, from the first paragraph, first sentence of the passage.

8. A

The white blood cell count can indicate disease (cancer). We know this from the last sentence of paragraph two, "The physical properties of white blood cells, such as volume, conductivity, and granularity, changes due to the presence of immature cells, or malignant cells."

9. B

The general tone is informal.

10. B

The statement, " Fewer people have aquariums in their office than at home," cannot be inferred from this article.

11. C

The author does not provide evidence for this statement.

12. B

The following statement is an opinion, " Aquarium gravel improves the aesthetics of the aquarium."

13. A

This is a triumphant speech where President Kennedy is celebrating his victory.

14. C

The statement, "We dare not forget today that we are the heirs of that first revolution" is an opinion.

15. C

This question tests the reader's vocabulary skills. The uses of the negatives "but" and "less," especially right next to each other, may confuse readers into answering with options A or D, which list words that are antonyms to "militant." Readers may also be confused by the comparison of healthy people with what is being described as an overly healthy person--both people are good, but the reader may look for which one is "worse" in the comparison, and therefore stray toward the antonym words. One key to understanding the meaning of "militant" if the reader is unfamiliar with it is to look at the root of the word; readers can then easily associate it with "military" and gain a sense of what the word signifies: defense (especially considered that the immune system defends the body). Option C is correct over option B because "militant" is an adjective, just as the words in option C are, whereas the words in option B are nouns.

16. C

This question tests the reader's understanding of function within writing. The other options are all details included surrounding the quoted text, and may therefore confuse the reader. A somewhat contradicts what is said earlier in the paragraph, which is that tests and treatments are improving, and probably doctors are along with them, but the paragraph doesn't actually mention doctors, and the subject of the question is the medicine. Option B may seem correct to readers who aren't careful to understand that, while the author does mention the large number of people affected, the author is touching on the realities of living with allergies rather about the likelihood of curing all allergies. Similarly, while the author does mention the "balance" of the body, which is easily associated with "wholesome," the author is not really making an argument and especially is not making an extreme statement that allergy medicines should be outlawed. Again, because the article's tone is on living with allergies, option C is an appropriate choice that fits with the title and content of the text.

17. B

This question tests the reader's inference skills. The text does not state who is doing the recommending, but the use of the "patients," as well as the general context of the passage, lends itself to the logical partner, "doctors," B. The author does mention the recommendation but doesn't present it as her own (i.e. "I recommend that"), so option A may be eliminated. It may seem plausible that allergy people with allergies (option D) may be recommend medicines or products to other people with allergies, but the text does not necessarily support this interaction taking place. Option C may be selected because the EpiPen is specifically mentioned, but the use of the phrase "such as" when it is introduced is not limiting enough to assume the recommendation is coming from its creators.

18. D

This question tests the reader's global understanding of the text. Option D includes the main topics of the three body paragraphs, and isn't too focused on a specific aspect or quote from the text, as the other questions are, giving a skewed summary of what the author intended. The reader may be drawn to option B because of the title of the passage and the use of words like "better," but the message of the passage is larger and more general than this.

19. C

This question tests the reader's summarization skills. The use of the word "actually" in describing what kind of people poets are, as well as other moments like this, may lead readers to selecting options B or D, but the author is more information than trying to persuade readers. The author gives no indication that she loves poetry (option B) or that people, students specifically (D), should write poems. Option A is incorrect because the style and content of this paragraph do not match those of a foreword; forewords usually focus on the history or ideas of a specific poem to introduce it more fully and help it stand out against other poems. The author here focuses on several poems and gives broad statements. Instead, she tells a kind of story about poems, giving three very broad time periods in which to discuss them, thereby giving a brief history of poetry, as option C states.

20. A

This question tests the reader's summarization skills. Key words in the topic sentences of each of the paragraphs ("oldest", "Renaissance", "modern") should give the reader an idea that the author is moving chronologically. The opening and closing sentence-paragraphs are broad and talk generally. B seems reasonable, but epic poems are mentioned in two paragraphs, eliminating the idea that only new types of poems are used in each paragraph. Option C is also easily eliminated because the author clearly mentions several different poets, groups of people, and poems. Option D also seems reasonable, considering that the author does move from older forms of poetry to newer forms, but use of "so (that)" makes this statement false, for the author gives no indication that she is rushing (the paragraphs are about the same size) or that she prefers modern poetry.

21. D
This question tests the reader's attention to detail. The key word is "invented"--it ties together the Mesopotamians, who invented the written word, and the fact that they, as the inventors, also invented and used poetry. The other selections focus on other details mentioned in the passage, such as that the Renaissance's admiration of the Greeks (option C) and that Beowulf is in Old English (option A). Option B may seem like an attractive answer because it is unlike the others and because the idea of heroes seems rooted in ancient and early civilizations.

22. B
This question tests the reader's vocabulary and contextualization skills. "Telling" is not an unusual word, but it may be used here in a way that is not familiar to readers, as an adjective rather than a verb in gerund form. A may seem like the obvious answer to a reader looking for a verb to match the use they are familiar with. If the reader understands that the word is being used as an adjective and that option A is a ploy, they may opt to select option D, "wordy," but it does not make sense in context. Option C can be easily eliminated, and doesn't have any connection to the paragraph or passage. "Significant" (option B) makes sense contextually, especially relative to the phrase "give insight" used later in the sentence.

23. B
This question tests the reader's summarization skills. Option A is a very broad statement that may or may not be true, and seems to be in context, but has nothing to do with the passage. The author does mention that the statue was probably used on a temple dedicated to the Greek gods (option D), but in no way discusses or argues for the gods' attitude toward or claim on these temples or its faucets. Nike does indeed lead the gods into a war (the Titan war), as option C suggests, but this is not mentioned by the passage and students who know this may be drawn to this answer but have not done a close enough analysis of the text that is

actually in the passage. Option B is appropriately expository, and connects the titular emphasis to the idea that the Greek gods are very important to Greek culture.

24. C

This question tests the reader's summarization skills. The test for question C is pulled straight from the paragraph, but is not word for word, so it may seem too obvious to be the right answer. The passage does talk about Nike being the goddess of war, as A states, but the third paragraph only touches on it and it is an inference that soldiers destroyed the statue, when this question is asking specifically for what the third paragraph actually stated. Option B is also straight from the text, with a minor but key change: the inclusion of the words "all" and "never" are too limiting and the passage does not suggest that these limits exist. If the reader selects option D, they are also making an inference that is misguided for this type of question. The paragraph does state that the arms and head are "lost" but does not suggest who lost them.

25. A

This question tests the reader's ability to recognize function in writing. Option B can be eliminated based on the purpose of the passage, which is expository and not persuasive. The author may or may not feel this way, but the passage does not show evidence of being argumentative for that purpose. Options C and D are both details found in the text, but neither encompasses the entire message of the passage, which has an overall message of learning about culture from art and making guesses about how the two are related, as suggested by option A.

Help with Reading Comprehension

At first sight, reading comprehension tests look challenging especially if you are given long essays to answer only two to three questions. While reading, you might notice your attention wandering, or you may feel sleepy. Do not be discouraged because there are various tactics and long range strategies that make comprehending even long, boring essays easier.

Your friends before your foes. It is always best to tackle essays or passages with familiar subjects rather than those with unfamiliar ones. This approach applies the same logic as tackling easy questions before hard ones. Skip passages that do not interest you and leave them for later when there is more time left.

Don't use 'special' reading techniques. This is not the time for speed-reading or anything like that – just plain ordinary reading – not too slow and not too fast.

Read through the entire passage and the questions before you do anything. Many students try reading the questions first and then looking for answers in the passage thinking this approach is more efficient. What these students do not realize is that it is often hard to navigate in unfamiliar roads. If you do not familiarize yourself with the passage first, looking for answers become not only time-consuming but also dangerous because you might miss the context of the answer you are looking for. If you read the questions first you will only confuse yourself and lose valuable time.

Familiarize yourself with reading comprehension questions. If you are familiar with the common types of reading questions, you are able to take note of important parts of the passage, saving time. There are six major kinds of reading questions.

- **Main Idea**- Questions that ask for the central thought or significance of the passage.

• **Specific Details** - Questions that asks for explicitly stated ideas.

• **Drawing Inferences** - Questions that ask for a statement's intended meaning.

• **Tone or Attitude** - Questions that test your ability to sense the emotional state of the author.

• **Context Meaning** – Questions that ask for the meaning of a word depending on the context.

• **Technique** – Questions that ask for the method of organization or the writing style of the author.

Read. Read. Read. The best preparation for reading comprehension tests is always to read, read and read. If you are not used to reading lengthy passages, you will probably lose concentration. Increase your attention span by making a habit out of reading.

Reading Comprehension tests become less daunting when you have trained yourself to read and understand fast. Always remember that it is easier to understand passages you are interested in. Do not read through passages hastily. Make mental notes of ideas that you think might be asked.

Reading Strategy

When facing the reading comprehension section of a standardized test, you need a strategy to be successful. You want to keep several steps in mind:

• **First, make a note of the time and the number of sections**. Time your work accordingly. Typically, four to five minutes per section is sufficient. Second, read the directions for each selection thoroughly before beginning (and listen well to any additional verbal instructions, as they will often clarify obscure or confusing written guidelines). You must know exactly how to do what you're about to do!

- **Now you're ready to begin reading the selection**. Read the passage carefully, noting significant characters or events on a scratch sheet of paper or underlining on the test sheet. Many students find making a basic list in the margins helpful. Quickly jot down or underline one-word summaries of characters, notable happenings, numbers, or key ideas. This will help you better retain information and focus wandering thoughts. Remember, however, that your main goal in doing this is to find the information that answers the questions. Even if you find the passage interesting, remember your goal and work fast but stay on track.

- **Now read the question and all of the choices.** Now you have read the passage, have a general idea of the main ideas, and have marked the important points. Read the question and all of the choices. Never choose an answer without reading them all! Questions are often designed to confuse – stay focussed and clear. Usually the answer choices will focus on one or two facts or inferences from the passage. Keep these clear in your mind.

- **Search for the answer**. With a very general idea of what the different choices are, go back to the passage and scan for the relevant information. Watch for big words, unusual or unique words. These make your job easier as you can scan the text for the particular word.

- **Mark the Answer**. Now you have the key information the question is looking for. Go back to the question, quickly scan the choices and mark the correct one.

Understand and practice the different types of standardized reading comprehension tests. See the list above for the different types. Typically, there will be several questions dealing with facts from the selection, a couple more inference questions dealing with logical consequences of those facts, and periodically an application-oriented question surfaces to force you to make connections with what you already know. Some students prefer to answer the questions as listed, and feel classifying the question and then ordering is wasting precious time. Other students prefer to answer the different types of questions in order of how easy or difficult they are. The choice is yours and do whatever works for you. If you want to try answering in order of difficulty, here is a recommended order, answer fact questions first; they're easily found within the passage. Tackle inference problems next, after re-reading the question(s) as many times as you need to. Application or 'best guess' questions usually take the longest, so save them for last.

Use the practice tests to try out both ways of answering and see what works for you.

For more help with reading comprehension, see Multiple Choice Secrets book at www.multiple choice.ca.

Main Idea and Supporting Details

Identifying the main idea, topic and supporting details in a passage can feel like an overwhelming task. The passages used for standardized tests can be boring and seem difficult - Test writers don't use interesting passages or ones that talk about things most people are familiar with. Despite these obstacles, all passages and paragraphs will have the information you need to answer the questions.

The topic of a passage or paragraph is its subject. It's the general idea and can be summed up in a word or short phrase. On some standardized tests, there is a short description of the passage if it's taken from a longer work. Make sure you read the description as it might state the topic of the passage. If not, read the passage and ask yourself, "Who or what is this about?" For example:

Over the years, school uniforms have been hotly debated. Arguments are made that students have the right to show individuality and express themselves by choosing their own clothes. However, this brings up social and academic issues. Some kids cannot afford to wear the clothes they like and might be bullied by the "better dressed" students. With attention drawn to clothes and the individual, students will lose focus on class work and the reason they are in school. School uniforms should be mandatory.

Ask: What is this paragraph about?

Topic: school uniforms

Once you have the topic, it's easier to find the main idea. The main idea is a specific statement telling what the writer wants you to know about the topic. Writers usually state the main idea as a thesis statement. If you're looking for the main idea of a single paragraph, the main idea is called the topic sentence and will probably be the first or last sentence. If you're looking for the main idea of an entire passage, look for the thesis statement in either the first or last paragraph. The main idea is usually restated in the conclusion. To find the main idea of a passage or paragraph, follow these steps:

1. Find the topic.

2. Ask yourself, "What point is the author trying to make about the topic?"

3. Create your own sentence summarizing the author's point.

4. Look in the text for the sentence closest in meaning to yours.

Look at the example paragraph again. It's already established that the topic of the paragraph is school uniforms. What is the main idea/topic sentence?

Ask: "What point is the author trying to make about school uniforms?"

Summary: Students should wear school uniforms.

Topic sentence: School uniforms should be mandatory.

Main Idea: School uniforms should be mandatory.

Each paragraph offers supporting details to explain the main idea. The details could be facts or reasons, but they will always answer a question about the main idea. What? Where? Why? When? How? How much/many? Look at the example paragraph again. You'll notice that more than one sentence answers a question about the main idea. These are the supporting details.

Main Idea: School uniforms should be mandatory.

Ask: Why? Some kids cannot afford to wear clothes they like and could be bullied by the "better dressed" kids. Supporting Detail

With attention drawn to clothes and the individual, Students will lose focus on class work and the reason they are in school. Supporting Detail

What if the author doesn't state the main idea in a topic sentence? The passage will have an implied main idea. It's not as difficult to find as it might seem. Paragraphs are always organized around ideas. To find an implied main idea, you need to know the topic and then find the relationship between the supporting details. Ask yourself, "What is the point the author is making about the relationship between the details?".

> Cocoa is what makes chocolate good for you. Chocolate comes in many varieties. These delectable flavors include milk chocolate, dark chocolate, semi-sweet, and white chocolate.

Ask: What is this paragraph about?
Topic: Chocolate
Ask: What? Where? Why? When? How? How much/many?

Supporting details: Chocolate is good for you because it is made of cocoa, Chocolate is delicious, Chocolate comes in different delicious flavors

Ask: What is the relationship between the details and what is the author's point?

Main Idea: Chocolate is good because it is healthy and it tastes good.

Testing Tips for Main Idea Questions

1. Skim the questions – not the answer choices - before reading the passage.

2. Questions about main idea might use the words "theme", "generalization", or "purpose".

3. Save questions about the main idea for last. On standardized tests like the SAT, the answers to the rest of the questions can be found in order in the passage.

3. Underline topic sentences in the passage. Most tests allow you to write in your testing booklet.

4. Answer the question in your own words before looking at the answer choices. Then match your answer with an answer choice.

5. Cross out incorrect answer choices immediately to prevent confusion.

6. If two of the answer choices mean the same thing but use different words, they are BOTH incorrect.

7. If a question asks about the whole passage, cross out the answer choices that apply to only part of it.

8. If only part of the information is correct, that answer choice is incorrect.

9. An answer choice that is too broad is incorrect. All information needs to be backed up by the passage.

10. Answer choices with extreme wording are usually incorrect.

Drawing Inferences And Conclusions

Drawing inferences and making conclusions happens all the time. In fact, you probably do it every time you read—sometimes without even realizing it! For example, remember the first time you saw the movie "The Lion King." When you meet Scar for the first time, he is trapping a helpless mouse with his sharp claws preparing to eat it. When you see this action you guess that Scar is going to be the bad character in the movie. Nothing appeared to tell you this. No caption came across the bottom of the screen that said "Bad Guy." No red arrow pointed to Scar and said "Evil Lion." No, you made an inference about his character based on the context clue you were given. You do the same thing when you read!

When you draw an inference or make a conclusion you are doing the same thing—you are making an educated guess based on the hints the author gives you. We call these hints "context clues." Scar trapping the innocent mouse is the context clue about Scar's character.

Usually you are making inferences and drawing conclusions the entire time you are reading. Whether you realize it or not, you are constantly making educated guesses based on context clues. Think about a time you were reading a book and something happened that you were expecting to happen. You're not psychic! Actually, you were picking up on the context clues and making inferences about what was going to happen next!

Let's try an easy example. Read the following sentences and answer the questions at the end of the passage.

> Shelly really likes to help people. She loves her job because she gets to help people every single day. However, Shelly has to work long hours and she can get called in the middle of the night for emergencies. She wears a white lab coat at work and usually she carries a stethoscope.

What is Shelly's job?

    a. Musician

    b. Lawyer

    c. Doctor

    d. Teacher

This probably seemed easy. Drawing inferences isn't always this simple, but it is the same basic principle. How did you know Shelly was a doctor? She helps people, she works long hours, she wears a white lab coat, and she gets called in for emergencies at night. Context Clues! Nowhere in the paragraph did it say Shelly was a doctor, but you were able to draw that conclusion based on the information provided in the paragraph.

There is a catch, though. Remember that when you draw inferences based on reading, you should only use the information given to you by the author. Sometimes it is easy for us to make conclusions based on knowledge that is already in our mind—but that can lead you to drawing an incorrect inference. For example, let's pretend there is a bully at your school named Brent. Now let's say you read a story and the main character's name is Brent. You could NOT infer that the character in the story is a bully just because his name is Brent. You should only use the information given to you by the author to avoid drawing the wrong conclusion.

Let's try another example.

> Social media is an extremely popular new form of connecting and communicating over the internet. Since Facebook's original launch in 2004, millions of people have joined in the social media craze. In fact, it is estimated that almost 75% of all internet users aged 18 and older use some form of social media. Facebook started at Harvard University as a way to get students connected. However, it quickly grew into a worldwide phenomenon and today, the founder of Facebook, Mark Zuckerberg has an estimated net worth of 28.5 billion dollars.

Facebook is not the only social media platform, though. Other sites such as Twitter, Instagram, and Snapchat have since been invented and are quickly becoming just as popular! Many social media users actually use more than one type of social media. Furthermore, most social media sites have created mobile apps that allow people to connect via social media virtually anywhere in the world!

What is the most likely reason that other social media sites like Twitter and Instagram were created?

> a. Professors at Harvard University made it a class project.
>
> b. Facebook was extremely popular and other people thought they could also be successful by designing social media sites.
>
> c. Facebook was not connecting enough people.
>
> d. Mark Zuckerberg paid people to invent new social media sites because he wanted lots of competition.

Here, the correct answer is B. Facebook was extremely popular and other people thought they could also be successful by designing social media sites. How do we know this? What are the context clues? Take a look at the first paragraph. What do we know based on this paragraph?

Well, one sentence refers to Facebook's original launch. This suggests that Facebook was one of the first social media sites. In addition, we know that the founder of Facebook has been extremely successful and is worth billions of dollars. From this we can infer that other people wanted to imitate Facebook's idea and become just as successful as Mark Zuckerberg.

Let's go through the other answers. If you chose A, it might be because Facebook started at Harvard University, so you drew the conclusion that all other social media sites were also started at Harvard University. However, there is no mention of class projects, professors, or students designing social media. So there doesn't seem to be enough support for choice A.

If you chose C, you might have been drawing your own conclusions based on outside information. Maybe none of your friends are on Facebook, so you made an inference that Facebook didn't connect enough people, so more sites were invented. Or maybe you think the people who connect on Facebook are too old, so you don't think Facebook connects enough people your age. This might be true, but remember inferences should be drawn from the information the author gives you!

If you chose D, you might be using the information that Mark Zuckerberg is worth over 28 billion dollars. It would be easy for him to pay others to design new sites, but remember, you need to use context clues! He is very wealthy, but that statement was giving you information about how successful Facebook was—not suggesting that he paid others to design more sites!

So remember, drawing inferences and conclusions is simply about using the information you are given to make an educated guess. You do this every single day so don't let this concept scare you. Look for the context clues, make sure they support your claim, and you'll be able to make accurate inferences and conclusions!

Meaning From Context

Often in Reading Comprehension questions, you are asked for the definition of a word, which you have to infer from the surrounding text, called "meaning in context." Here are a few examples with step-by-step solutions, and a few tips and tricks to answering meaning from context questions.

There are thousands of words in the English language. It is impossible for us to know what every single one of them means, but we also don't have time to Google a definition every time we read a word we don't understand! Even the smartest person in the world comes across words they don't know, but luckily we can use context clues to help us determine what things actually mean.

Context clues are really just little hints that can help us determine the meaning of words or phrases and honestly, the easiest way to learn how to use context clues is to practice!

Let's start with a few basic examples.

> In some countries many people are not given access to schools, teachers, or books. In these countries, people might be illiterate.

You might not know what the word illiterate means, but let's use the clues in the sentence to help us. If people are not given access to schools, teachers, or books, what might happen? They probably don't learn what we learned in school so they might not know some of the things that we learned from our teachers! Illiterate actually means "unable to read or write." This makes sense based on the context clues!

Let's work through another example.

> We have so much technology today! So much technology that many people have started using tablets and computers to read ebooks instead of paper books! In fact, some of these people actually think that reading paper books is archaic!

Let's look for the context clues. Well, what do we know from this paragraph? We have a lot of technology and sometimes people read ebooks instead of paper books. From this we can draw the conclusion that ebooks are beginning to replace paper books because ebooks are newer and better. So if ebooks are newer and better, it must mean that paper books are older. Archaic actually means "very old or old-fashioned," which again we determined from the context clues.

Let's see if you can try a few on your own now.

Cody noticed the strawberries in his refrigerator were old and moldy, so he abstained and threw them away.

What does abstained most likely mean?

    a. chose not to consume

    b. washed

    c. shared

    d. cut into pieces

The correct answer here is A. The context clues told you the strawberries were old and moldy, and that Cody did something and then threw them away. If the strawberries were moldy, and Cody abstained, it makes sense that he didn't eat them—which is choice A.

You may have chosen choice B. If the strawberries were old and moldy, Cody could have washed them. But use ALL of the context clues. After he abstained, he threw them away. Why would Cody wash them and then throw them away? That doesn't make sense! In addition, why would he share them if they were old and moldy? Finally, I suppose Cody could have cut them into pieces, but why would he need to do that before throwing them away? It doesn't make as much sense, so choice A is the correct answer!

Let's do one more.

Scott had disdain for Lily ever since she lied to their boss and got him fired.

    a. Compassion

    b. Hate

    c. Remorse

    d. Money

The correct answer is B. Scott was fired because Lily lied. Can you imagine if this happened to you? I think you would have some pretty strong feelings just like Scott!

By understanding the context, you can determine the meaning of even the hardest of words!

Point Of View And Purpose

You may not think so, but everything you read was written for a purpose. Now, it might not be the most exciting purpose, but regardless of whether it's a website, a magazine article, a book, or even a Facebook status—everything is written for a particular purpose. By understanding that purpose and the author's point of view, we can better comprehend what we read!

To determine the purpose of a written piece, you are asking yourself a very easy question. Why was this written? Usually the answer will be one of these three choices:

1. To inform
2. To persuade
3. To entertain.

First, you should ask yourself if the piece is fiction or non-fiction. Fiction is a type of writing that is not true. It is imaginary, made-up, or theoretical. For example, Harry Potter is fiction. While reading, it may seem like this world of wizards exists, but in reality, there is no Hogwarts or Diagon Alley. It is imaginary. Can you guess which purpose fiction has? Correct, choice 3—to entertain! So if you can tell if a piece is fiction or non-fiction, you can begin to narrow down the author's purpose!

Now, if a piece is non-fiction you are left with choice 1 or 2. To inform or to persuade. Here's another trick. If the piece is simply giving you INFORMation, the author's purpose is most likely to inform you! Think of an example of an informational piece you've read recently. Textbooks, most newspaper articles, how-to blogs, the instruction manual for your new cell phone, all these are great examples where the author's purpose was to inform you.

Some nonfiction pieces, though, are written to persuade you—meaning they are trying to convince you to do something or believe something. Can you think of a few examples where the author's purpose was to persuade?

When an author's purpose is to persuade you, they will have a point of view. What side is the author on? What are they trying to convince you to believe or do? Understanding a point of view will help you better understand the author's purpose.

Let's try a few examples. Determine what the author's purpose is for each of the following:

1. A packet that explains how to use an Xbox One

2. A story where a student plays Xbox One every day and becomes the youngest person to invent an Xbox One game.

3. An article that discusses the dangers of Xbox One and says nobody should ever play.

All three of these examples have similar information—Xbox One. However, the author has a different purpose in each.

Number 1 is simply to inform. It is giving you INFORMation. Number 2 is to entertain. It is a fiction story based on imagination, not facts. Number 3 is to persuade—the author is trying to convince readers that Xbox One is bad and people should stop playing.

Now that we have a better understanding of purpose, let's dive into point of view a little deeper. Read the passage below and answer the questions.

Mac computers are better than PC Computers. Mac computers are more expensive, but they are worth every penny. They are made better than PC computers and typically last longer. They have better software programs and almost never get viruses or break down. PC computers have to get fixed or replaced all the time and it ends up being more expensive than just buying a Mac computer in the first place! Plus, Mac computers are more user friendly and they will sync with your Ipad and Iphone! I highly suggest getting a Mac if you are looking to buy a new computer.

What was the author's purpose when they wrote this paragraph?

a. Inform

b. Persuade

c. Entertain

Right, you should have chosen B, to persuade. The author has an opinion, which suggests they are persuading you to do something.

What is the author's point of view?

a. PC Computers are the best computers to buy

b. Both Mac's and PC's are great computers if you take care of them

c. Mac Computers are better than PC Computers

d. Everybody should own tablets rather than computers

The correct answer is C. The author clearly thinks that Mac computers are better than PC's. This is their point of view, or what side of the argument they are on! By understanding the author's purpose and point of view, you can better understand what you read. Just remember, everything was written for a purpose! Once you understand that purpose, you can better comprehend what point the author is trying to make!

Mathematics

THIS SECTION CONTAINS A SELF-ASSESSMENT AND MATH TUTORIALS. The tutorials are designed to familiarize general principals and the self-assessment contains general questions similar to the math questions likely to be on the COMPASS® exam, but are not intended to be identical to the exam questions. The tutorials are not designed to be a complete math course, and it is assumed that students have some familiarity with math. If you do not understand parts of the tutorial, or find the tutorial difficult, it is recommended that you seek out additional instruction.

Tour of the COMPASS Mathematics Content

Below is a list of the likely mathematics topics likely to appear on the COMPASS®. Make sure that you understand these topics.

Basic Mathematics

- Convert decimals, percent, and fractions

- Solve word problems

- Calculate percent and ratio

- Operations using fractions, percent and fractions

- Simple geometry and measurement

- Estimation

Algebra

- Operations with polynomials

- Exponents

- Solving Inequalities

- Linear equations with one and two variables

- Solving quadratics

College Level Math

- Coordinate geometry

- Trigonometry

- Solutions of inequalities

- Logarithms

- Sequences

The questions in the self-assessment are not the same as you will find on the COMPASS® - that would be too easy! And nobody knows what the questions will be and they change all the time. Mostly, the changes consist of substituting new questions for old, but the changes also can be new question formats or styles, changes to the number of questions in each section, changes to the time limits for each section, and combining sections. So, while the format and exact wording of the questions may differ slightly, and changes from year to year, if you can answer the questions below, you will have no problem with the mathematics section of the COMPASS®.

Mathematics Self-Assessment

The purpose of the self-assessment is:

- Identify your strengths and weaknesses.

- Develop your personalized study plan (above)

- Get accustomed to the COMPASS® format

- Extra practice – the self-assessments are almost a full 3rd practice test!

- Provide a baseline score for preparing your study schedule.

Since this is a Self-assessment, and depending on how confident you are with mathematics, timing yourself is optional.

Once complete, use the table below to assess your understanding of the content, and prepare your study schedule described in chapter 1.

80% - 100%	Excellent – you have mastered the content
60 – 79%	Good. You have a working knowledge. Even though you can just pass this section, you may want to review the tutorials and do some extra practice to see if you can improve your mark.
40% - 59%	Below Average. You do not understand the content. Review the tutorials , and retake this quiz again in a few days, before proceeding to the practice test questions.

Less than 40%	Poor. You have a very limited understanding. Please review the tutorials , and retake this quiz again in a few days, before proceeding to the practice test questions.

Mathematics Self-Assessment Answer Sheet

1. Ⓐ Ⓑ Ⓒ Ⓓ
2. Ⓐ Ⓑ Ⓒ Ⓓ
3. Ⓐ Ⓑ Ⓒ Ⓓ
4. Ⓐ Ⓑ Ⓒ Ⓓ
5. Ⓐ Ⓑ Ⓒ Ⓓ
6. Ⓐ Ⓑ Ⓒ Ⓓ
7. Ⓐ Ⓑ Ⓒ Ⓓ
8. Ⓐ Ⓑ Ⓒ Ⓓ
9. Ⓐ Ⓑ Ⓒ Ⓓ
10. Ⓐ Ⓑ Ⓒ Ⓓ
11. Ⓐ Ⓑ Ⓒ Ⓓ
12. Ⓐ Ⓑ Ⓒ Ⓓ
13. Ⓐ Ⓑ Ⓒ Ⓓ
14. Ⓐ Ⓑ Ⓒ Ⓓ
15. Ⓐ Ⓑ Ⓒ Ⓓ
16. Ⓐ Ⓑ Ⓒ Ⓓ
17. Ⓐ Ⓑ Ⓒ Ⓓ

18. Ⓐ Ⓑ Ⓒ Ⓓ
19. Ⓐ Ⓑ Ⓒ Ⓓ
20. Ⓐ Ⓑ Ⓒ Ⓓ
21. Ⓐ Ⓑ Ⓒ Ⓓ
22. Ⓐ Ⓑ Ⓒ Ⓓ
23. Ⓐ Ⓑ Ⓒ Ⓓ
24. Ⓐ Ⓑ Ⓒ Ⓓ
25. Ⓐ Ⓑ Ⓒ Ⓓ
26. Ⓐ Ⓑ Ⓒ Ⓓ
27. Ⓐ Ⓑ Ⓒ Ⓓ
28. Ⓐ Ⓑ Ⓒ Ⓓ
29. Ⓐ Ⓑ Ⓒ Ⓓ
30. Ⓐ Ⓑ Ⓒ Ⓓ
31. Ⓐ Ⓑ Ⓒ Ⓓ
32. Ⓐ Ⓑ Ⓒ Ⓓ
33. Ⓐ Ⓑ Ⓒ Ⓓ
34. Ⓐ Ⓑ Ⓒ Ⓓ

35. Ⓐ Ⓑ Ⓒ Ⓓ
36. Ⓐ Ⓑ Ⓒ Ⓓ
37. Ⓐ Ⓑ Ⓒ Ⓓ
38. Ⓐ Ⓑ Ⓒ Ⓓ
39. Ⓐ Ⓑ Ⓒ Ⓓ
40. Ⓐ Ⓑ Ⓒ Ⓓ
41. Ⓐ Ⓑ Ⓒ Ⓓ
42. Ⓐ Ⓑ Ⓒ Ⓓ
43. Ⓐ Ⓑ Ⓒ Ⓓ
44. Ⓐ Ⓑ Ⓒ Ⓓ
45. Ⓐ Ⓑ Ⓒ Ⓓ

Basic Math Self-Assessment

1. Brad has agreed to buy everyone a Coke. Each drink costs $1.89, and there are 5 friends. Estimate Brad's cost.

    a. $7

    b. $8

    c. $10

    d. $12

2. Sarah weighs 25 pounds more than Tony. If together they weigh 205 pounds, how much does Sarah weigh approximately in kilograms? Assume 1 pound = 0.4535 kilograms.

    a. 41

    b. 48

    c. 50

    d. 52

3. A building is 15 m long and 20 m wide and 10 m high. What is the volume of the building?

    a. 45 m³

    b. 3,000 m³

    c. 1500 m³

    d. 300 m³

4. 15 is what percent of 200?

    a. 7.5%

    b. 15%

    c. 20%

    d. 17.50%

5. A boy has 5 red balls, 3 white balls and 2 yellow balls. What percent of the balls are yellow?

    a. 2%

    b. 8%

    c. 20%

    d. 12%

6. Convert 4/20 to percent.

    a. 25%

    b. 20%

    c. 40%

    d. 30%

7. Convert 0.55 to percent.

    a. 45%

    b. 15%

    c. 75%

    d. 55%

8. A man buys an item for $420 and has a balance of $3000.00. How much did he have before?

    a. $2,580

    b. $3,420

    c. $2,420

    d. $342

9. What is the best approximate solution for 1.135 - 113.5?

    a. -110

    b. 100

    c. -90

    d. 110

10. Solve 3/4 + 2/4 + 1.2

    a. 1 1/7

    b. 2 3/4

    c. 2 9/20

    d. 3 1/4

11. The average weight of 13 students in a class of 15 (two were absent that day) is 42 kg. When the remaining two are weighed, the average became 42.7 kg. If one of the remaining students weighs 48 kg., how much does the other weigh?

    a. 44.7 kg.

    b. 45.6 kg.

    c. 46.5 kg.

    d. 47.4 kg.

12. The total expense of building a fence around a square-shaped field is $2000 at a rate of $5 per meter. What is the length of one side?

    a. 40 meters

    b. 80 meters

    c. 100 meters

    d. 320 meters

13. There were some oranges in a basket. By adding 8/5 of the total to the basket, the new total is 130. How many oranges were in the basket?

    a. 60

    b. 50

    c. 40

    d. 35

14. 3 boys are asked to clean a surface that is 4 ft². If the surface is divided equally among the boys, how much will each clean?

    a. 1 ft 6 inches²

    b. 14 inches²

    c. 1 ft 2 inches²

    d. 16 inches²

15. A person earns $25,000 per month and pays $9,000 income tax per year. The Government increased income tax by 0.5% per month and his monthly earning was increased $11,000. How much more income tax will he pay per month?

    a. $1260

    b. $1050

    c. $750

    d. $510

16. Estimate 2009 x 108

    a. 110,000

    b. 2,0000

    c. 21,000

    d. 210,000

Exponents

17. Express in 3^4 standard form

    a. 81

    b. 27

    c. 12

    d. 9

18. Simplify $4^3 + 2^4$

    a. 45

    b. 108

    c. 80

    d. 48

19. If $x = 2$ and $y = 5$, solve $xy^3 - x^3$

    a. 240

    b. 258

    c. 248

    d. 242

20. $X^3 \times X^2 =$

    a. 5^x

    b. x^{-5}

    c. x^{-1}

    d. X^5

21. Express 100000^0 in standard form.

    a. 1

    b. 0

    c. 100000

    d. 1000

22. Solve $\sqrt{144}$

    a. 14

    b. 72

    c. 24

    d. 12

Linear Equations

23. Solve the linear equation: -x - 7 = -3x - 9

    a. -1

    b. 0

    c. 1

    d. 2

24. Solve the system: 4x - y = 5   x + 2y = 8

    a. (3,2)

    b. (3,3)

    c. (2,3)

    d. (2,2)

Polynomials

25. Add $-3x^2 + 2x + 6$ and $-x^2 - x - 1$.

    a. $-2x^2 + x + 5$

    b. $-4x^2 + x + 5$

    c. $-2x^2 + 3x + 5$

    d. $-4x^2 + 3x + 5$

26. Simplify the following expression:

$3x^3 + 2x^2 + 5x - 7 + 4x^2 - 5x + 2 - 3x^3$

    a. $6x^2 - 9$

    b. $6x^2 - 5$

    c. $6x^2 - 10x - 5$

    d. $6x^2 + 10x - 9$

27. Multiply x - 1 and x² + x + 2.

    a. $x^3 + x - 2$

    b. $x^2 + x - 2$

    c. $x^3 + x^2 - 2$

    d. $x^3 + 2x^2 - 2$

28. Factor the polynomial 9x² - 6x + 12.

    a. $3(x^2 - 2x + 9)$

    b. $3(3x^2 - 3x + 4)$

    c. $9(x^2 - 3x + 3)$

    d. $3(3x^2 - 2x + 4)$

Quadratics

29. Find 2 numbers that sum to 21 and the sum of the squares is 261.

    a. 14 and 7

    b. 15 and 6

    c. 16 and 5

    d. 17 and 4

30. Using the factoring method, solve the quadratic equation: x² + 4x + 4 = 0

    a. 0 and 1

    b. 1 and 2

    c. 2

    d. -2

31. Using the quadratic formula, solve the quadratic equation: x - 31/x = 0

         a. $-\sqrt{13}$ and $\sqrt{13}$

         b. $-\sqrt{31}$ and $\sqrt{31}$

         c. $-\sqrt{31}$ and $2\sqrt{31}$

         d. $-\sqrt{3}$ and $\sqrt{3}$

32. Using the factoring method, solve the quadratic equation: $2x^2 - 3x = 0$

         a. 0 and 1.5

         b. 1.5 and 2

         c. 2 and 2.5

         d. 0 and 2

33. Using the quadratic formula, solve the quadratic equation: $x^2 - 9x + 14 = 0$

         a. 2 and 7

         b. -2 and 7

         c. -7 and -2

         d. -7 and 2

Geometry

34. What is the perimeter of the above shape?

    a. 12 cm
    b. 16 cm
    c. 6 cm
    d. 20 cm

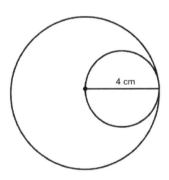

35. What is (area of large circle) - (area of small circle) in the figure above?

    a. 8π cm^2
    b. 10π cm^2
    c. 12π cm^2
    d. 16π cm^2

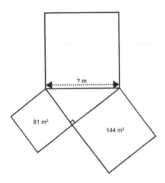

36. What is the length of each side of the indicated square above?

    a.   10
    b.   15
    c.   20
    d.   5

Trigonometry

37. If sides a and b of a right triangle are 8 and 6, respectively, find cosine of a.

    a. 1/5
    b. 5/3
    c. 3/5
    d. 2/5

38. Find tangent of a of a right triangle, if a is 3 and b is 5.

    a. 1/4
    b. 5/3
    c. 4/3
    d. 3/4

39. If a=300, find sin300 + cos600.

    a. 1/2

    b. 2/3

    c. 1

    d. 3/2

Inequalities

40. Solve the inequality: -7x - 1 ≥ 13

    a. $(2, + \infty)$

    b. $(7, + \infty)$

    c. $(-\infty, -2)$

    d. $(2, + \infty)$

41. Solve the inequality: 2x - 1 ≥ x + 10

    a. $(-\infty, 9)$

    b. $(9, +\infty)$

    c. $(-\infty, -9)$

    d. $(11, +\infty)$

Logarithms

42. If $\log_2 x = 3$, then x is:

    a. 9

    b. 8

    c. 7

    d. 6

43. Solve the equation $\log_4 1/4 = x$.

    a. -1

    b. 0

    c. 1

    d. 2

Sequences

44. If $a_0 = 3$ and $a_n = -a_{n-1} + 3$, find a_3 of the sequence $\{a_n\}$.

    a. 0

    b. 1

    c. 2

    d. 3

45. If terms of the sequence $\{a_n\}$ are represented by $a_n = a_{n-1}/n$ and $a_1 = 1$, find a_4.

    a. 1/2

    b. 1/4

    c. 1/16

    d. 1/24

Answer Key

1. C
If there are 5 friends and each drink costs $1.89, we can round up to $2 per drink and estimate the total cost at, 5 X $2 = $10.
The actual cost is 5 X $1.89 = $9.45.

2. D
If we subtract 25 pounds from total 205, then in the remaining 180 pounds, their weights are equal, at 90 pounds each.
So Sarah's weight will be = 90 + 25 = 115 pounds.
In kilograms it will be = 115×0.4535 = 52.15 Kg.
Sarah will weigh about 52 Kg.

3. B
Formula for volume of a shape is L x W x H = 15 x 20 x 10 = 3,000 m³

4. A
15/200 = X/100
200X = (15 * 100)
1500/20 Cancel zeroes in the numerator and denominator
15/2 = 7.5%.

Notice that the questions asks, What 15 is what percent of 200? The question does not ask, what is 15% of 200! The answers are very different.

5. C
Total no. of balls = 10, no. of yellow balls = 2, answer = 2/10 X 100 = 20%.

6. B
4/20 X 100 = 1/5 X 100 = 20%

7. D
0.55 X 100 = 55%

8. B
(Amount Spent) $420 + $3000 (Balance) = $3420

9. A
1.135 - 113.5 = -112.37. Best approximate = -110

10. C
3/4 + 2/4 + 1.2, first convert the decimal to fraction, = 3/4 + 2/4 + 1 1/5 = ¾ + 2/4 + 6/5 = (find common denominator)

(15 + 10 + 24)/20 = 49/20 = 2 9/20

11. C
Total weight of 13 students with average 42 will be = 42 × 13 = 546 kg.
Total weight of 15 students with average 42.7 will be = 42.7 × 15 = 640.5 kg. So total weight of the remaining 2 will be = 640.5 - 546 = 94.5 kg. Weight of the other will be = 94.5 – 48 = 46.5 kg

12. C
First use the total cost to calculate the perimeter (the sum of all four sides). Total length of the fence will be = 2000/5 = 400 meters. This will equal to the perimeter of the square field, so the length of one side will be = 400/4 = 100 meters.

13. B
Let the number of oranges in the basket before additions = x
Then: X + 8x/5 = 130
5x + 8x = 650
650 = 13x
X = 50

14. D
First convert to inches – 4 X 12 = 48 sq. in. 48/3 = 16 sq. in.

15. D
With the new tax rate, income tax is 3.5% so the per month income tax = $9000/12 = $750. Per month income tax rate = $750 X 100/$25,000 = 3%. Income per month = $25,000 + $11,000 = $36,000. Monthly tax amount = $36,000 X 0.035 = $1260

Amount of addition tax = $1260 - $750 = $510.

16. D
2009 x 108 = 210,000

Answer Key

Exponents

17. A
3 x 3 x 3 x 3 = 81

18. C
(4 x 4 x 4) + (2 x 2 x 2 x 2) = 64 + 16 = 80

19. D
$2(5)^3 - (2)^3$ = 2(125) – 8 = 250 – 8 = 242

20. D
X^3 x X^2 = X^{3+2} = X^5
To multiply exponents with like bases, add the exponents.

21. A
Any value (except 0) raised to the power of 0 equals 1.

22. D
$\sqrt{144}$ = 12

Linear Equations

23. A
-x - 7 = -3x - 9
-x + 3x = -9 + 7
2x = -2
x = (-2)/2
x = -1

24. C
(2, 3)
4x - y = 5
x + 2y = 8
y = 4x - 5

x + 2(4x - 5) = 8
x + 8x - 10 = 8
x + 8x - 10 = 8
9x = 10 + 8
9x = 18
x = 2

Use solution, x = 2 to find y.

y = (4 * 2) - 5
y = 8 - 5
y = 3

Polynomials

25. B
$-4x^2 + x + 5$
$(-3x^2 + 2x + 6) + (-x^2 - x - 1)$
$-3x^2 + 2x + 6 - x^2 - x - 1$
$-4x^2 + x + 5$

26. B
$6x^2 - 5$
$3x^3 + 2x^2 + 5x - 7 + 4x^2 - 5x + 2 - 3x^3 = 6x^2 - 5$

27. A
$x^3 + x - 2$
$(x - 1)(x^2 + x + 2) = x^3 + x^2 + 2x - x^2 - x - 2 = x^3 + x - 2$

28. D
$3(3x^2 - 2x + 4)$
$9x^2 - 6x + 12 = 3 * 3x^2 - 2 * 3x + 3 * 4 = 3(3x^2 - 2x + 4)$

Quadratics

29. B
The numbers are 15 and 6.
x + 7 = 21 => x = 21 -7
$x^2 + y^2 = 261$

$(21 - 7)^2 + y^2 = 261$
$441 - 42y + y^2 + y^2 = 261$
$2y^2 - 42y + 180 = 0$
$y^2 - 21y + 90 = 0$
$y_{1,2} = 21 \pm \sqrt{441 - 360}/2$
$y_{1,2} = 21 \pm \sqrt{81}/2$
$y_{1,2} = 21 \pm 9/2$
$y_1 = 15$
$y_2 = 6$
$x_1 = 21 = y_1 = 21 - 15 = 6$
$x_2 = 21 - y_2 = 21 - 6 = 15$

30. D
-2

$$x^2 + 4x + 4 = 0$$

$$x^2 + 2x + 2x + 4 = 0$$

$$x(x+2) + 2(x+2) = 0$$

$$(x+2)(x+2) = 0$$

$$(x+2)^2 = 0$$

$$x = -2$$

31. B
$-\sqrt{31}$ and $\sqrt{31}$

$$x - \frac{31}{x} = 0$$

$$\frac{x^2 - 31}{x} = 0 \Rightarrow x^2 - 31 = 0$$

$$x_{1,2} = \frac{0 \pm \sqrt{-4 \cdot (-31)}}{2}$$

$$x_{1,2} = \frac{\pm 2\sqrt{31}}{2}$$

$$x_{1,2} = \pm\sqrt{31}$$

$$x_1 = \sqrt{31}$$

$$x_2 = -\sqrt{31}$$

32. A
0 and 1.5
$2x^2 - 3x = 0$
$x(2x - 3)$
x = 0 or 2x - 3 = 0
x = 0 or x = 3/2
x = 0 or x = 1.5

33. A
2 and 7

$$x^2 - 9x + 14 = 0$$

$$x_{1,2} = \frac{-(-9) \pm \sqrt{(-9)^2 - 4 \cdot 14}}{2 \cdot 1}$$

$$x_{1,2} = \frac{9 \pm \sqrt{81 - 56}}{2}$$

$$x_{1,2} = \frac{9 \pm \sqrt{25}}{2}$$

$$x_{1,2} = \frac{9 \pm 5}{2}$$

$$x_1 = \frac{9 + 5}{2} = 7$$

$$x_2 = \frac{9 - 5}{2} = 2$$

Geometry

34. B
The square with 2 cm side common to the rectangle apart from 4 cm side. So the perimeter = 2 + 2 + 2 + 4 + 2 + 4 = 16 cm.

35. C
Given: Two circles with a smaller circle (diameter given) exactly half the larger circle (radius given).
Difference = (Area of large circle) - (Area of small large circle)
$\pi \, 4^2 - \pi \, 2^2$
= $16\pi - 4\pi$
Difference = 12π cm^2

36. B
Pythagorean Theorem:
(Hypotenuse)^2 = (Perpendicular)^2 + (Base)^2
$h^2 = a^2 + b^2$

$a^2 = 81$, $b^2 = 144$
$h^2 = a^2 + b^2$
$h^2 = 81+144$
$h^2 = 225$
$h = 15$

Trigonometry

37. C 3/5
$a = 8$
$b = 6$
$a^2 + b^2 = c^2$
$82 + 62 = c^2$
$64 + 36 = c^2$
$c^2 = 100$
$c = 10$
$\cos a = b/c = 6/10 = 3/5$

38. D 3/4
$a = 3$
$c = 5$
$a^2 + b^2 = c^2$
$32 + b^2 = 52$
$b^2 = 25 - 9$
$b^2 = 16$
$b = 4$
$tg a = a/b = 3/4$

39. C 1
$a=30^0$
$\sin 30^0 + \cos 60^0 = 1/2 + 1/2 = 1$

Inequalities

40. C $(-\infty, -2)$

$-7x - 1 \geq 13$
$-7x \geq 13 + 1$
$-7x \geq 14$
$-x \geq 2/(-1)$
$x \leq -2$

41. D
$2x - 1 \geq x + 10$
$2x - x \geq 10 + 1$
$x \geq 11$

Logarithms

42. B 8
$\log_2 x = 3$
$23 = x$
$x = 8$

43. A -1
$\log_4 1/4 = x.$
$4x = 1/4$
$4x = 4-1$
$x = -1$

Sequences

44. A 0
$a_0 = 3$
$a_n = - a_{n-1} + 3$
$a_1 = - a_0 + 3 = -3 + 3 = 0$
$a_2 = -a_1 + 3 = 0 + 3 = 3$
$a_3 = -a_2 + 3 = -3 + 3 = 0$

45. D $1/24$

$a_n = a_{n-1}/n$

$a_1 = 1$

$a_2 = a_1/2 = 1/2$

$a_3 = a_2/3 = (1/2)/3 = 1/6$

$a_4 = a_3/4 = (1/6)/4 = 1/24$

Fraction Tips, Tricks and Shortcuts

When you are writing an exam, time is precious, and anything you can do to answer faster is a real advantage. Here
are some ideas, shortcuts, tips and tricks that can speed up
answering fractions problems.

Remember that a fraction is just a number which names
a portion of something. For instance, instead of having a
whole pie, a fraction says you have a part of a pie--such as
a half of one or a fourth of one.

Two digits make up a fraction. The digit on top is known
as the numerator. The digit on the bottom is known as the
denominator. To remember which is which, just remember
that "denominator" and "down" both start with a "d." And
the "downstairs" number is the denominator. So for instance, in ½, the numerator is the 1 and the denominator
(or "downstairs") number is the 2.

- It's easy to add two fractions if they have the same
  denominator. Just add the digits on top, and leave
  the bottom one the same: 1/10 + 6/10 = 7/10.

- It's the same with subtracting fractions with the
  same denominator: 7/10 - 6/10 = 1/10.

- Adding and subtracting fractions with different denominators is a little more complicated. First, you
  have to get the problem so that they do have the
  same denominators. The easiest way to do this is to
  multiply the denominators: For 2/5 + 1/2 multiply
  5 by 2. Now you have a denominator of 10. But now
  you have to change the top numbers too. Since you
  multiplied the 5 in 2/5 by 2, you also multiply the
  2 by 2, to get 4. So the first number is now 4/10.
  Since you multiplied the second number times 5, you
  also multiply its top number by 5, to get a final fraction of 5/10. Now you can add 5 and 4 together to
  get a final sum of 9/10.

- Sometimes you'll be asked to reduce a fraction to
  its simplest form. This means getting it to where the

only common factor of the numerator and denominator is 1. Think of it this way: Numerators and denominators are brothers that must be treated the same. If you do something to one, you must do it to the other, or it's just not fair. For instance, if you divide your numerator by 2, then you should also divide the denominator by the same. Let's take an example: The fraction 2/10 . This is not reduced to its simplest terms because there is a number that will divide evenly into both: the number 2. We want to make it so that the only number that will divide evenly into both is 1. What can we divide into 2 to get 1? The number 2, of course! Now to be "fair," we have to do the same thing to the denominator: Divide 2 into 10 and you get 5. So our new, reduced fraction is 1/5.

☐ In some ways, multiplying fractions is the easiest of all: Just multiply the two top numbers and then multiply the two bottom numbers. For instance, with this problem:
2/5 X 2/3 you multiply 2 by 2 and get a top number of 4; then multiply 5 by 3 and get a bottom number of 15. Your answer is 4/15.

☐ Dividing fractions is more involved, but still not too hard. You once again multiply, but only AFTER you have turned the second fraction upside-down. To divide ⅞ by ½, turn the ½ into 2/1, then multiply the top numbers and multiply the bottom numbers: ⅞ X 2/1 gives us 14 on top and 8 on the bottom.

Converting Fractions to Decimals

There are a couple of ways to become good at converting fractions to decimals. The fastest way is to memorize some basic fraction facts. Here are fractions that you should know:

1/100 is "one hundredth," expressed as a decimal, it's .01.

1/50 is "two hundredths," expressed as a decimal, it's .02.

1/25 is "one twenty-fifths" or "four hundredths," expressed as a decimal, it's .04.

1/20 is "one twentieth" or ""five hundredths," expressed as a decimal, it's .05.

1/10 is "one tenth," expressed as a decimal, it's .1.

1/8 is "one eighth," or "one hundred twenty-five thousandths," expressed as a decimal, it's .125.

1/5 is "one fifth," or "two tenths," expressed as a decimal, it's .2.

1/4 is "one fourth" or "twenty-five hundredths," expressed as a decimal, it's .25.

1/3 is "one third" or "thirty-three hundredths," expressed as a decimal, it's .33.

1/2 is "one half" or "five tenths," expressed as a decimal, it's .5.

3/4 is "three fourths," or "seventy-five hundredths," expressed as a decimal, it's .75.

Of course, if you're no good at memorization, another good technique for converting a fraction to a decimal is to manipulate it so that the fraction's denominator is 10, 100, 1000, or some other power of 10. Here's an example: We'll start with 3/4. What is the first number in the 4 "times table" that you can multiply and get a multiple of 10? Can you multiply 4 by something to get 10? No. Can you multiply it by something to get 100? Yes! 4 X 25 is 100. So let's take that 25 and multiply it by the numerator in our fraction ¾. The numerator is 3, and 3 X 25 is 75. We'll move the decimal in 75 all the way to the left, and we find that ¾ is .75.

We'll do another one: 1/5. Again, we want to find a power of 10 that 5 goes into evenly. Will 5 go into 10? Yes! It goes 2 times. So we'll take that 2 and multiply it by our numerator, 1, and we get 2. We move the decimal in 2 all the way to the left and find that 1/5 is equal to .2.

Converting Fractions to Percent

Working with either fractions or percents can be intimidating enough. But converting from one to the other? That's a genuine nightmare for those who are not math wizards. But really, it doesn't have to be that way. Here are two ways to make it easier and faster to convert a fraction to a percent.

☐ First, you might remember that a fraction is nothing more than a division problem: you're dividing the bottom number into the top number. So for instance, if we start with a fraction 1/10, we are making a division problem with the 10 on the outside the bracket and the 1 on the inside. As you remember from your lessons on dividing by decimals, since 10 won't go into 1, you add a decimal and make it 10 into 1.0. 10 into 10 goes 1 time, and since it's behind the decimal, it's .1. And how do we say .1? We say "one tenth," which is exactly what we started with: 1/10. So we have a number we can work with now: .1. When we're dealing with percents, though, we're dealing strictly with hundredths (not tenths). You remember from studying decimals that adding a zero to the right of the number on the right side of the decimal does not change the value. Therefore, we can change .1 into .10 and have the same number--except it's expressed as hundredths. We have 10 hundredths. That's ten out of 100--which is just another way of saying ten percent (ten per hundred or ten out of 100). In other words .1 = .10 = 10 percent. Remember, if you're changing from a decimal to a percent, get rid of the decimal on the left and replace it with a percent mark on the right: 10%. Let's review those steps again: Divide 10 into 1. Since 10 doesn't go into 1, turn 1 into 1.0. Now divide 10 into 1.0. Since 10 goes into 10 1 time, put it there and add your decimal to make it .1. Since a percent is always "hundredths," let's change .1 into .10. Then remove the decimal on the left and replace with a percent sign on the right. The answer is 10%.

☐ If you're doing these conversions on a multiple-choice test, here's an idea that might be even easier and faster. Let's say you have a fraction of 1/8 and you're asked what the percent is. Since we know that "percent" means hundredths, ask yourself what number we can multiply 8 by to get 100. Since there is no number, ask what number gets us close to 100. That number is 12: 8 X 12 = 96. So it gets us a little less than 100. Now, whatever you do to the denominator, you have to do to the numerator. Let's multiply 1 X 12 and we get 12. However, since 96 is a little less than 100, we know that our answer will be a percent a little MORE than 12%. So if your possible answers on the multiple-choice test are these:

a) 8.5%   b) 19%   c)12.5%   d) 25%

then we know the answer is c) 12.5%, because it's a little MORE than the 12 we got in our math problem above.

Another way to look at this, using multiple choice strategy is you know the answer will be "about" 12. Looking at the other choices, they are all too large or too small and can be eliminated right away.

This was an easy example to demonstrate, so don't be fooled! You probably won't get such an easy question on your exam, but the principle holds just the same. By estimating your answer quickly, you can eliminate choices immediately and save precious exam time.

Decimal Tips, Tricks and Shortcuts

Converting Decimals to Fractions

One of the most important tricks for correctly converting a decimal to a fraction doesn't involve math at all. It's simply to learn to say the decimal correctly. If you say "point one" or "point 25" for .1 and .25, you'll have more trouble getting the conversion correct. However, if you know that it's called "one tenth" and "twenty-five hundredths," you're on the way to a correct conversion. That's because, if you know your fractions, you know that "one tenth" looks like this: 1/10. And "twenty-five hundredths" looks like this: 25/100.

Even if you have digits before the decimal, such as 3.4, learning how to say the word will help you with the conversion into a fraction. It's not "three point four," it's "three and four tenths." Knowing this, you know that the fraction which looks like "three and four tenths" is 3 4/10.

Of course, your conversion is not complete until you reduce the fraction to its lowest terms: It's not 25/100, but 1/4.

Converting Decimals to Percent

Changing a decimal to a percent is easy if you remember one math formula: multiply by 100. For instance, if you start with .45, you change it to a percent by simply multiplying it by 100. You then wind up with 45. Add the % sign to the end and you get 45%.

That seems easy enough, right? Think of it this way: You just take out the decimal and stick in a percent sign on the opposite sign. In other words, the decimal on the left is replaced by the % on the right.

It doesn't work that easily if the decimal is in the middle of the number. Let's use 3.7 for example. Take out the decimal in the middle and replace it with a 0 % at the end. So 3.7 converted to decimal is 370%.

Percent Tips, Tricks and Shortcuts

Percent problems are not nearly as scary as they appear, if you remember this neat trick:

Draw a cross as in:

Portion	Percent
Whole	100

In the upper left, write PORTION. In the bottom left, write WHOLE. In the top right, write PERCENT and in the bottom right, write 100. Whatever your problem is, you will leave blank the unknown, and fill in the other four parts. For example, let's suppose your problem is: Find 10% of 50. Since we know the 10% part, we put 10 in the percent corner. Since the whole number in our problem is 50, we put that in the corner marked whole. You always put 100 underneath the percent, so we leave it as is, which leaves only the top left corner blank. This is where we'll put our answer. Now simply multiply the two corner numbers that are NOT 100. Here, it's 10 X 50. That gives us 500. Now multiply this by the remaining corner, or 100, to get a final answer of 5. 5 is the number that goes in the upper-left corner, and is your final solution.

Another hint to remember: Percents are the same thing as hundredths in decimals. So .45 is the same as 45 hundredths or 45 percent.

Converting Percents to Decimals

Percent are simply a specific type of decimals, so it should be no surprise that converting between the two is actually simple. Here are a few tricks and shortcuts to keep in mind:

☐ Remember that percent literally means "per 100" or "for every 100." So when you speak of 30% you are saying 30 for every 100 or the fraction 30/100. In basic math, you learned fractions that have 10 or 100 as the denominator can easily be turned into a decimal. 30/100 is thirty hundredths, or expressed as a decimal, .30.

☐ Another way to look at it: To convert a percent to a decimal, simply divide the number by 100. So for instance, if the percent is 47%, divide 47 by 100. The result will be .47. Get rid of the % mark and you're done.

☐ Remember that the easiest way of dividing by 100 is by moving your decimal two spots to the left.

Converting Percents to Fractions

Converting percents to fractions is easy. After all, a percent is nothing except a type of fraction; it tells you what part of 100 that you're talking about. Here are some simple ideas for making the conversion from a percent to a fraction:

☐ If the percent is a whole number -- say 34% -- then simply write a fraction with 100 as the denominator (the bottom number). Then put the percentage itself on top. So 34% becomes 34/100.

☐ Now reduce as you would reduce any percent. In this case, by dividing 2 into 34 and 2 into 100, you get 17/50.

☐ If your percent is not a whole number -- say 3.4% --then convert it to a decimal expressed as hundredths. 3.4 is the same as 3.40 (or 3 and forty hundredths). Now ask yourself how you would express "three and forty hundredths" as a fraction. It would, of course, be 3 40/100. Reduce this and it becomes 3 2/5.

How to Solve Word Problems

Most students find math word problems difficult. Tackling word problems is much easier if you have a systematic approach which we outline below.

Here is the biggest tip for studying word problems.

Practice regularly and systematically. Sounds simple and easy right? Yes it is, and yes it really does work.

Word problems are a way of thinking and require you to translate a real word problem into mathematical terms.

Some math instructors go so far as to say that learning how to think mathematically is the main reason for teaching word problems.

So what do we mean by Practice regularly and systematically? Studying word problems and math in general requires a logical and mathematical frame of mind. The only way that you can get this is by practicing regularly, which means everyday.

It is critical that you practice word problems everyday for the 5 days before the exam as a bare minimum.

If you practice and miss a day, you have lost the mathematical frame of mind and the benefit of your previous practice is pretty much gone. Anyone who has done any number of math tests will agree – you have to practice everyday.

Everything is important. The other critical point about word problems is that all the information given in the problem has some purpose. There is no unnecessary information! Word problems are typically around 50 words in 1 to 3 sentences. If the sometimes complicated relationships are to be explained in that short an explanation, every word has to count. Make sure that you use every piece of information.

Here are 9 simple steps to solve word problems.

Step 1 – Read through the problem at least three times. The first reading should be a quick scan, and the next two readings should be done slowly to answer these important questions:

What does the problem ask? (Usually located towards the end of the problem)

What does the problem imply? (This is usually a point you were asked to remember).

Mark all information, and underline all important words or

phrases.

Step 2 – Try to make a pictorial representation of the problem such as a circle and an arrow to show travel. This makes the problem a bit more real and sensible to you.

A favorite word problem is something like, 1 train leaves Station A travelling at 100 km/hr and another train leaves Station B travelling at 60 km/hr. ...

Draw a line, the two stations, and the two trains at either end. This will solidify the situation in your mind.

Step 3 – Use the information you have to make a table with a blank portion to show information you do not know.

Step 4 – Assign a single letter to represent each unknown datum in your table. You can write down the unknown that each letter represents so that you do not make the error of assigning answers for the wrong unknown, because a word problem may have multiple unknowns and you will need to create equations for each unknown.

Step 5 – Translate the English terms in the word problem into a mathematical algebraic equation. Remember that the main problem with word problems is that they are not expressed in regular math equations. Your ability to correctly identify the variables and translate the word problem into an equation determines your ability to solve the problem.

Step 6 – Check the equation to see if it looks like regular equations that you are used to seeing and whether it looks sensible. Does the equation appear to represent the information in the question? Take note that you may need to rewrite some formulas needed to solve the word problem equation. For example, word distance problems may need you rewriting the distance formula, which is Distance = Time x Rate. If the word problem requires that you solve for time you will need to use Distance/Rate and Distance/Time to solve for Rate. If you understand the distance word problem you should be able to identify the variable you need to solve for.

Step 7 – Use algebra rules to solve the derived equation. Take note that the laws of equation demands that what is done on this side of the equation has to also be done on the other side. You have to solve the equation so that the unknown ends alone on one side. Where there are multiple unknowns you will need to use elimination or substitution methods to resolve all the equations.

Step 8 – Check your final answers to see if they make sense with the information given in the problem. For example if the word problem involves a discount, the final price should be less or if a product was taxed then the final answer has to cost more.

Step 9 – Cross check your answers by placing the answer or answers in the first equation to replace the unknown or unknowns. If your answer is correct then both side of the equation must equate or equal. If your answer is not correct then you may have derived a wrong equation or solved the equation wrongly. Repeat the necessary steps to correct.

Types of Word Problems

Word problems can be classified into 12 types. Below are examples of each type with a complete solution. Some types of word problems can be solved quickly using multiple choice strategies and some cannot. Always look for ways to estimate the answer and then eliminate choices.

1. Age

A girl is 10 years older than her brother. By next year, she will be twice the age of her brother. What are their ages now?

    a. 25, 15

    b. 19, 9

    c. 21, 11

    d. 29, 19

Solution: B

We will assume that the girl's age is "a" and her brother's age is "b". This means that based on the information in the first sentence,
a = 10 + b

Next year, she will be twice her brother's age, which gives, a + 1 = 2(b+1)

We need to solve for one unknown factor and then use the answer to solve for the other. To do this we substitute the value of "a" from the first equation into the second equation. This gives

10+b + 1 = 2b + 2
11 + b = 2b + 2
11 – 2 = 2b – b
b= 9

9 = b this means that her brother is 9 years old. Solving for the girl's age in the first equation gives a = 10 + 9. a = 19 the girl is aged 19. So, the girl is aged 19 and the boy is 9

2. Distance or speed

Two boats travel down a river towards the same destination, starting at the same time. One boat is traveling at 52 km/hr, and the other boat at 43 km/hr. How far apart will they be after 40 minutes?

    a. 46.67 km

    b. 19.23 km

    c. 6 km

    d. 14.39 km

Solution: C

After 40 minutes, the first boat will have traveled = 52 km/hr x 40 minutes/60 minutes = 34.66 km
After 40 minutes, the second boat will have traveled = 43 km/hr x 40/60 minutes = 28.66 km

Difference between the two boats will be 34.6 km – 28.66 km = 6 km.

Multiple Choice Strategy

First estimate the answer. The first boat is travelling 9 km. faster than the second, for 40 minutes, which is 2/3 of an hour. 2/3 of 9 = 6, as a rough guess of the distance apart.

Choices A, B and D can be eliminated right away.

3. Ratio

The instructions in a cookbook state that 700 grams of flour must be mixed in 100 ml of water, and 0.90 grams of salt added. A cook however has just 325 grams of flour. What is the quantity of water and salt that he should use?

    a. 0.41 grams and 46.4 ml

    b. 0.45 grams and 49.3 ml

    c. 0.39 grams and 39.8 ml

    d. 0.25 grams and 40.1 ml

Solution: A

The Cookbook states 700 grams of flour, but the cook only has 325. The first step is to determine the percentage of flour he has 325/700 x 100 = 46.4%
That means that 46.4% of all other items must also be used.
46.4% of 100 = 46.4 ml of water
46.4% of 0.90 = 0.41 grams of salt.

Multiple Choice Strategy

The recipe calls for 700 grams of flour but the cook only has 325, which is just less than half, the quantity of water and salt are going to be about half.

Choices C and D can be eliminated right away.   Choice B is very close so be careful.   Looking closely at Choice B, it is exactly half, and since 325 is slightly less than half of 700, it can't be correct.

Choice A is correct.

4. Percent

An agent received $6,685 as his commission for selling a property. If his commission was 13% of the selling price, how much was the property?

    a. $68,825
    b. $121,850
    c. $49,025
    d. $51,423

Solution: D

Let's assume that the property price is x
That means from the information given, 13% of x = 6,685
Solve for x,
x = 6685 x 100/13 = $51,423

Multiple Choice Strategy

The commission,13%, is just over 10%, which is easier to work with. Round up $6685 to $6700, and multiple by 10 for an approximate answer. 10 X 6700 = $67,000. You can do this in your head. Choice B is much too big and can be eliminated. Choice C is too small and can be eliminated. Choices A and D are left and good possibilities.

Do the calculations to make the final choice.

5. Sales & Profit

A store owner buys merchandise for $21,045. He transports them for $3,905 and pays his staff $1,450 to stock the merchandise on his shelves. If he does not incur further costs, how much does he need to sell the items to make $5,000 profit?

    a. $32,500
    b. $29,350
    c. $32,400
    d. $31,400

Solution: D

Total cost of the items is $21,045 + $3,905 + $1,450 = $26,400
Total cost is now $26,400 + $5000 profit = $31,400

Multiple Choice Strategy

Round off and add the numbers up in your head quickly. 21,000 + 4,000 + 1500 = 26500. Add in 5000 profit for a total of 31500.

Choice B is too small and can be eliminated. Choice C and Choice A are too large and can be eliminated.

6. Tax/Income

A woman earns $42,000 per month and pays 5% tax on her monthly income. If the Government increases her monthly taxes by $1,500, what is her income after tax?

    a. $38,400
    b. $36,050
    c. $40,500
    d. $39, 500

Solution: A

Initial tax on income was 5/100 x 42,000 = $2,100
$1,500 was added to the tax to give $2,100 + 1,500 = $3,600
Income after tax is $42,000 - $3,600 = $38,400

7. Simple Interest Word Problems

Simple interest is one type of interest problems. There are always four variables of any simple interest equation. With simple interest, you would be given three of these variables and be asked to solve for one unknown variable. With more complex interest problems, you would have to solve for multiple variables.

The four variables of simple interest are:
P – Principal which refers to the original amount of money put in the account
I – Interest or the amount of money earned as interest
r – Rate or interest rate. This MUST ALWAYS be in decimal format and not in percentage
t – Time or the amount of time the money is kept in the account to earn interest

The formula for simple interest is I = P x r x t

Example 1

A customer deposits $1,000 in a savings account with a bank that offers 2% interest. How much interest will be earned after 4 years?

For this problem, there are 3 variables as expected.

P = $1,000
t = 4 years
r = 2%
I = ?

Before we can begin solving for I using the simple interest formula, we need to first convert the rate from percentage to decimal.

2% = 2/100 = 0.02

Now we can use the formula: I = P x r x t

I = 1,000 x 0.02 x 4 = 80
This means that the $1,000 would have earned an interest of $80 after 4 years. The total in the account after 4 years will thus be principal + interest earned, or 1,000 + 80 = $1,080

Example 2

Sandra deposits $1400 in a savings account with a bank at 5% interest. How long will she have to leave the money in the bank to earn $420 as interest to buy a second-hand car?

In this example, the given information is:
I = $420
P = $1,400
r - 5%
t - ?
As usual, first we convert the rate from percentage to decimal
5% = 5/100 = 0.05

Next, we plug in the variables we know into the simple interest formula - I = P x r x t

420 = 1,400 x 0.05 x t
420 = 70 x t
420 = 70t
t = 420/70
t = 6

Sandra will have to leave her $1,400 in the bank for 6 years to earn her an interest of $420 at a rate of 5%.

Other important simple interest formula to remember

To use this formula below, do not convert r (rate) to decimal.

P = 100 x interest/ r x t
r = 100 x interest/p x t
t = 100 x interest/ p x r

8. Averaging

The average weight of 10 books is 54 grams. 2 more books were added and the average weight became 55.4. If one of the 2 new books added weighed 62.8 g, what is the weight of the other?

    a. 44.7 g
    b. 67.4 g
    c. 62 g
    d. 52 g

Solution: C

Total weight of 10 books with average 54 grams will be=10×54=540 g
Total weight of 12 books with average 55.4 will be=55.4×12=664.8 g
So total weight of the remaining 2 will be= 664.8 – 540 = 124.8 g
If one weighs 62.8, the weight of the other will be= 124.8 g – 62.8 g = 62 g

Multiple Choice Strategy

Averaging problems can be estimated by looking at which direction the average goes. If additional items are added and the average goes up, the new items much be greater than the average. If the average goes down after new items are added, the new items must be less than the average.

Here, the average is 54 grams and 2 books are added which increases the average to 55.4, so the new books must weight more than 54 grams.
Choices A and D can be eliminated right away.

9. Probability

A bag contains 15 marbles of various colors. If 3 marbles are white, 5 are red and the rest are black, what is the probability of randomly picking out a black marble from the bag?

    a. 7/15
    b. 3/15
    c. 1/5
    d. 4/15

Solution: A

Total marbles = 15
Number of black marbles = 15 – (3 + 5) = 7
Probability of picking out a black marble = 7/15

10. Two Variables

A company paid a total of $2850 to book for 6 single rooms and 4 double rooms in a hotel for one night. Another company paid $3185 to book for 13 single rooms for one night in the same hotel. What is the cost for single and double rooms in that hotel?

    a. single= $250 and double = $345
    b. single= $254 and double = $350
    c. single = $245 and double = $305
    d. single = $245 and double = $345

Solution: D

We can determine the price of single rooms from the information given of the second company. 13 single rooms = 3185.
One single room = 3185 / 13 = 245
The first company paid for 6 single rooms at $245. 245 x 6 = $1470
Total amount paid for 4 double rooms by first company = $2850 - $1470 = $1380
Cost per double room = 1380 / 4 = $345

11. Geometry

The length of a rectangle is 5 in. more than its width. The perimeter of the rectangle is 26 in. What is the width and length of the rectangle?

    a. width = 6 inches, Length = 9 inches
    b. width = 4 inches, Length = 9 inches
    c. width =4 inches, Length = 5 inches
    d. width = 6 inches, Length = 11 inches

Solution: B

Formula for perimeter of a rectangle is 2(L + W)
p=26, so 2(L+W) = p
The length is 5 inches more than the width, so
2(w+5) + 2w = 26

2w + 10 + 2w = 26
2w + 2w = 26 - 10
4w = 18

W = 16/4 = 4 inches

L is 5 inches more than w, so L = 5 + 4 = 9 inches.

12. Totals and fractions

A basket contains 125 oranges, mangos and apples. If 3/5 of the fruits in the basket are mangos and only 2/5 of the mangos are ripe, how many ripe mangos are there in the basket?

    a. 30

    b. 68

    c. 55

    d. 47

Solution: A
Number of mangos in the basket is 3/5 x 125 = 75
Number of ripe mangos = 2/5 x 75 = 30

Ratios

In mathematics, a ratio is a relationship between two numbers of the same kind[1] (e.g., objects, persons, students, spoonfuls, units of whatever identical dimension), usually expressed as "a to b" or a:b, sometimes expressed arithmetically as a dimensionless quotient of the two[2] which explicitly shows how many times the first number contains the second (not necessarily an integer).[3] In layman's terms a ratio represents, simply, for every amount of one thing, how much there is of another thing. For example, suppose I have 10 pairs of socks for every pair of shoes then the ratio of shoes:socks would be 1:10 and the ratio of socks:shoes would be 10:1.

Notation and terminology

The ratio of numbers A and B can be expressed as:[4]
the ratio of A to B
A is to B
A:B

A rational number which is the quotient of A divided by B
The numbers A and B are sometimes called terms with A being the antecedent and B being the consequent.

The proportion expressing the equality of the ratios A:B and C:D is written A:B=C:D or A:B::C:D. this latter form, when spoken or written in the English language, is often expressed as
A is to B as C is to D.

Again, A, B, C, D are called the terms of the proportion. A and D are called the extremes, and B and C are called the means. The equality of three or more proportions is called a continued proportion.[5]
Ratios are sometimes used with three or more terms. The dimensions of a two by four that is ten inches long are 2:4:10.

Examples

The quantities being compared in a ratio might be physical quantities such as speed or length, or numbers of objects, or amounts of particular substances. A common example of the last case is the weight ratio of water to cement used in concrete, which is commonly stated as 1:4. This means that the weight of cement used is four times the weight of water used. It does not say anything about the total amounts of cement and water used, nor the amount of concrete being made. Equivalently it could be said that the ratio of cement to water is 4:1, that there is 4 times as much cement as water, or that there is a quarter (1/4) as much water as cement..
Older televisions have a 4:3 "aspect ratio", which means that the width is 4/3 of the height; modern widescreen TVs have a 16:9 aspect ratio.
Fractional

If there are 2 oranges and 3 apples, the ratio of oranges to apples is 2:3, and the ratio of oranges to the total number of pieces of fruit is 2:5. These ratios can also be expressed in fraction form: there are 2/3 as many oranges as apples, and 2/5 of the pieces of fruit are oranges. If orange juice concentrate is to be diluted with water in the ratio 1:4, then one part of concentrate is mixed with four parts of water, giving five parts total; the amount of orange juice concentrate is 1/4 the amount of water, while the amount of orange juice concentrate is 1/5 of the total liquid. In both ratios and fractions, it is important to be clear what is being compared to what, and beginners often make mistakes for this reason.

Number of terms

In general, when comparing the quantities of a two-quantity ratio, this can be expressed as a fraction derived from the ratio. For example, in a ratio of 2:3, the amount/size/volume/number of the first quantity will be that of the second quantity. This pattern also works with ratios with more than two terms. However, a ratio with more than two terms cannot be completely converted into a single fraction; a single fraction represents only one part of the ratio since a fraction can only compare two numbers. If the ratio deals with objects or amounts of objects, this is often expressed as "for every two parts of the first quantity there are three parts of the second quantity."

Percent and ratio

If we multiply all quantities involved in a ratio by the same number, the ratio remains valid. For example, a ratio of 3:2 is the same as 12:8. It is usual either to reduce terms to the lowest common denominator, or to express them in parts per hundred (percent).

If a mixture contains substances A, B, C & D in the ratio 5:9:4:2 then there are 5 parts of A for every 9 parts of B, 4 parts of C and 2 parts of D. As 5+9+4+2=20, the total mixture contains 5/20 of A (5 parts out of 20), 9/20 of B, 4/20 of C, and 2/20 of D. If we divide all numbers by the total

and multiply by 100, this is converted to percentages: 25%
A, 45% B, 20% C, and 10% D (equivalent to writing the ratio
as 25:45:20:10).

Proportion

If the two or more ratio quantities encompass all the quantities in a particular situation, for example two apples and
three oranges in a fruit basket containing no other types of
fruit, it could be said that "the whole" contains five parts,
made up of two parts apples and three parts oranges. Here,
or 40% of the whole are apples or 60% of the whole are oranges. This comparison of a specific quantity to "the whole"
is sometimes called a proportion. Proportions are sometimes
expressed as percentages as demonstrated above.

Reduction

Note that ratios can be reduced (as fractions are) by dividing
each quantity by the common factors of all the quantities.
This is often called "cancelling." As for fractions, the simplest
form is considered to be that in which the numbers in the
ratio are the smallest possible integers.

Thus, the ratio 40:60 may be considered equivalent in meaning to the ratio 2:3 within contexts concerned only with relative quantities.

Mathematically, we write: "40:60" = "2:3" (dividing both
quantities by 20).
Grammatically, we would say, "40 to 60 equals 2 to 3."
An alternative representation is: "40:60::2:3"
Grammatically, we would say, "40 is to 60 as 2 is to 3."
A ratio that has integers for both quantities and that can-
not be reduced any further (using integers) is said to be in
simplest form or lowest terms.
Sometimes it is useful to write a ratio in the form 1:n or n:1
to enable comparisons of different ratios.

For example, the ratio 4:5 can be written as 1:1.25 (dividing both sides by 4). Alternatively, 4:5 can be written as 0.8:1 (dividing both sides by 5). Where the context makes the meaning clear, a ratio in this form is sometimes written without the 1 and the colon, though, mathematically, this makes it a factor or multiplier. [11]

Exponents: Tips, Shortcuts & Tricks

Exponents seem like advanced math to most—like some mysterious code with a complicated meaning. In fact, though, an exponent is just short hand for saying that you're multiplying a number by itself two or more times. For instance, instead of saying that you're multiplying 5 x 5 x 5, you can show that you're multiplying 5 by itself 3 times if you just write 5^3 .We usually say this as "five to the third power" or "five to the power of three." In this example, the raised 3 is an "exponent," while the 5 is the "base." You can even use exponents with fractions. For instance, $1/2^3$ means you're multiplying 1/2 x 1/2 x 1/2. (The answer is 1/8). Some other helpful hints for working with exponents:

- Here's how to do basic multiplication of exponents. If you have the same number with a different exponent (For instance 5^3 X 5^2) just add the exponents and multiply the bases as usual. The answer, then, is 25^5 .
- This doesn't work, though, if the bases are different. For instance, in 5^3 X 3^2 we simply have to do the math the long way to figure out the final solution: 5 x 5 x 5, multiplying that result times the result for 3 X 3. (The answer is 1125).
- Looking at it from the opposite side, to divide two exponents with the same base (or bottom number), subtract the smaller exponent from the larger one. If we were dividing the problem above, we would subtract the 2 from the 3 to get 1. 5 to the power of 1 is simply 5.
- One time when thinking of exponents as merely

multiplication doesn't work is when the raised number is zero. Any number raised to the "zeroth" power is 1 (Not, as we tend to think, zero).

Number (x)	X^2	X^3
1	1	1
2	4	8
3	9	27
4	16	64
5	25	125
6	36	216
7	49	343
8	64	512
9	81	729
10	100	1000
11	121	1331
12	144	1728
13	169	2197
14	196	2744
15	225	3375
16	256	4096

Solving One-Variable Linear Equations

Linear equations with variable x is an equation with the following form:

$$ax = b$$

where a and b are real numbers. If a=0 and b is different from 0, then the equation has no solution.

Let's solve one simple example of a linear equation with one variable:

$$4x - 2 = 2x + 6$$

When we are given this type of equation, we are always moving variables to the one side, and real numbers to the other side of the equals sign. Always remember: if you are changing sides, you are changing signs. Let's move all variables to the left, and real number to the right side:

$4x - 2 = 2x + 6$
$4x - 2x = 6 + 2$
$2x = 8$
$x = 8/2$
$x = 4$

When $2x$ goes to the left it becomes $-2x$, and -2 goes to the right and becomes $+2$. After calculations, we find that x is 4, which is a solution of our linear equation.

Let's solve a little more complex linear equation:

$2x - 6/4 + 4 = x$
$2x - 6 + 16 = 4x$
$2x - 4x = -16 + 6$
$-2x = -10$
$x = -10/-2$
$x = 5$

We multiply whole equation by 4, to lose the fractional line. Now we have a simple linear equation. If we change sides, we change the signs.

Solving Two-Variable Linear Equations

If we have 2 or more linear equations with 2 or more variables, then we have a system of linear equations. The idea here is to express one variable using the other in one equation, and then use it in the second equation, so we get a linear equation with one variable. Here is an example:

$x - y = 3$
$2x + y = 9$

From the first equation, we express y using x.

y = x - 3

In the second equation, we write x-3 instead of y. And there we get a linear equation with one variable x.

2x + x - 3 = 9
3x = 9 + 3
3x = 12
x = 12/3
x = 4

Now that we found x, we can use it to find y.

y = x - 3
y = 4 - 3
y = 1

So, the solution of this system is (x,y) = (4,1).

Let's solve one more system using a different method:

Solve:

5x - 3y = 17
x + 3y = 11

5x - 3y + x + 3y = 17 - 11

Notice that we have -3y in the first equation and +3y in the second. If we add these 2, we get zero, which means we lose variable y. So, we add these 2 equations and we get a linear equation with one variable.

6x = 6
x = 1

Now that we have x, we use it to find y.

5 - 3y = 17

-3y = 17 - 5
-3y = 12
y = 12/(-3)
y = -4

Adding and Subtracting Polynomials

When we are adding or subtracting 2 or more polynomials, we have to first group the same variables (arguments) that have the same degrees and then add or subtract them. For example, if we have ax^3 in one polynomial (where a is some real number), we have to group it with bx^3 from the other polynomial (where b is also some real number). Here is one example with adding polynomials:

$(-x^2 + 2x + 3) + (2x^2 + 4x - 5) =$
$-x^2 + 2x + 3 + 2x^2 + 4x - 5 =$
$x^2 + 6x - 2$

We remove the brackets, and since we have a plus in front of every bracket, the signs in the polynomials don't change. We group variables with the same degrees. We have -1 + 2, which is 1 and that's how we got x^2. For the first degree, where we have 2 + 4 which is 6, and the constants (real numbers) where we have 3 - 5 which is -2.

The principle is the same with subtracting, only we have to keep in mind that a minus in front of the polynomial changes all signs in that polynomial. Here is one example:

$(4x^3 - x^2 + 3) - (-3x^2 - 10) =$
$4x^3 - x^2 + 3 + 3x^2 + 10 =$
$4x^3 + 2x^2 + 13$

We remove the brackets, and since we have a minus in front of the second polynomial, all signs in that polynomial change. We have -3 x 2 and with minus in front, it becomes a plus and same goes for -10.

Now we group the variables with same degrees: there is no

variable with the third degree in the second polynomial, so we just write 4 x 3. We group other variables the same way as adding polynomials.

Multiplying and Dividing Polynomials

If we have two polynomials that we need to multiply, then multiply each member of the first polynomial with each member of the second.   Let's see in one example how this works:

$(x-1)(x-2) = x^2 - 2x - x + 2 = x^2 - 3x + 2$

The first member of the first polynomial is multiplied with the first member of the second polynomial and then with the second member of the second polynomial. Continue the process with the second member of the first polynomial, then simplify.

To multiply more polynomials, multiply the first 2, then multiply that result with next polynomial and so on. Here is one example:

$(1 - x)(2 - x)(3 - x) = (2 - x - 2x + x^2)\ (3-x)$
$= (2 - 3x + x^2)\ (3 - x)$
$= 6 - 2x - 9x + 3x^2 + 3x^2 - x^3 = 6 - 11x + 6x^2 - x^3$

Simplifying Polynomials

Let's say we are given some expression with one or more variables, where we have to add, subtract and multiply polynomials. We do the calculations with variables and constants and then we group the variables with the appropriate degrees. As a result, we would get a polynomial. This process is called simplifying polynomials, where we go from a complex expression to a simple polynomial.

Example:

Simplify the following expression and arrange the degrees from bigger to smaller:

$4 + 3x - 2x^2 + 5x + 6x^3 - 2x^2 + 1 = 6x^3 - 4x^2 + 8x + 5$

We can have more complex expressions such as:

$(x + 5)(1 - x) - (2x - 2) = x - x^2 + 5 - 5x - 2x + 2 = -x^2 - 6x + 7$

Here, first we multiply the polynomials and then we subtract the result and the third polynomial.

Factoring Polynomials

If we have a polynomial that we want to write as multiplication of a real number and a polynomial or as a multiplication of 2 or more polynomials, then we are dealing with factoring polynomials.

Let's see an example for a simple factoring:

$12x^2 + 6x - 4 =$
$2 * 6x^2 + 2 * 3x - 2 * 2 =$
$2(6x^2 + 3x - 2)$

We look at every polynomial member as a product of a real number and a variable. Notice that all real numbers in the polynomial are even, so they have the same number (factor). We pull out that 2 in front of the polynomial, and we write what is left.

What if have a more complex case, where we can't find a factor that is a real number? Here is an example:

$x^2 - 2x + 1 =$
$x^2 - x - x + 1 =$
$x(x - 1) - (x - 1) =$

(x - 1) (x - 1)

We can write -2x as –x-x . Now we group first 2 members and we see that they have the same factor x, which we can pull in front of them. For the other 2 members, we pull the minus in front of them, so we can get the same binomial that we got with the first 2 members. Now we have that this binomial is the factor for x(x-1) and (x-1).

If we pull x-1 in front (underlined), from the first member we are left with x, and from the second we have -1.
And that is how we transform a polynomial into a product of 2 polynomials (in this case binomials).

Quadratic equations

A. Factoring

Quadratic equations are usually called second degree equations, which mean that the second degree is the highest degree of the variable that can be found in the quadratic equation. The form of these equations is:

$ax^2 + bx + c = 0$

where a, b and c are some real numbers.

One way for solving quadratic equations is the factoring method, where we transform the quadratic equation into a product of 2 or more polynomials. Let's see how that works in one simple example:

x2 + 2x = 0
x(x + 2) = 0
(x = 0) V (x + 2 = 0)
(x = 0 V (x + -2)

Notice that here we don't have parameter c, but this is still a quadratic equation, because we have the second degree of variable x. Our factor here is x, which we put in front and we

are left with x+2. The equation is equal to 0, so either x or x+2 are 0, or both are 0.
So, our 2 solutions are 0 and -2.

B. Quadratic formula

If we are unsure how to rewrite quadratic equations so we can solve it using factoring method, we can use the formula for quadratic equation:

$$x_{1,2} = \frac{-b \pm \sqrt{b^2 - 4ac}}{2a}$$

We write $x_{1,2}$ because it represents 2 solutions of the equation. Here is one example:

$$3x^2 - 10x + 3 = 0$$

$$x_{1,2} = \frac{-b \pm \sqrt{b^2 - 4ac}}{2a}$$

$$x_{1,2} = \frac{-(-10) \pm \sqrt{(-10)^2 - 4 \cdot 3 \cdot 3}}{2 \cdot 3}$$

$$x_{1,2} = \frac{10 \pm \sqrt{100 - 36}}{6}$$

$$x_{1,2} = \frac{10 \pm \sqrt{64}}{6}$$

$$x_{1,2} = \frac{10 \pm 8}{6}$$

$$x_1 = \frac{10 + 8}{6} = \frac{18}{6} = 3$$

$$x_2 = \frac{10 - 8}{6} = \frac{2}{6} = \frac{1}{3}$$

We see that a is 3, b is -10 and c is 3.
We use these numbers in the equation and do some calculations.

Notice that we have + and -, so x_1 is for + and x_2 is for -, and that's how we get 2 solutions.

Cartesian Plane, Coordinate Plane and Coordinate Grid

To locate dots and draw lines and curves, we use the coordinate plane. It also called Cartesian coordinate plane. It is a two-dimensional surface with a coordinate grid in it, which helps us to count the units. For the counting of those units, we use x-axis (horizontal scale) and y-axis (vertical scale).

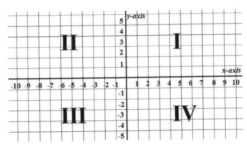

The whole system is called a coordinate system which is divided into 4 parts, called quadrants. The quadrant where all numbers are positive is the 1st quadrant (I), and if we go counterclockwise, we mark all 4 quadrants.

The location of a dot in the coordinate system is represented by coordinates. Coordinates are represented as a pair of numbers, where the 1st number is located on the x-axis and the 2nd number is located on the y-axis. So, if a dot A has coordinates a and b, then we write:

A=(a,b)   or   A(a,b)

The point where x-axis and y-axis intersect is called an origin. The origin is the point from which we measure the distance along the x and y axes.

In the Cartesian coordinate system we can calculate the distance between 2 given points. If we have dots with coordinates:
A=(a,b)
B=(c,d)

Then the distance d between A and B can be calculated by the following formula:

$$d = \sqrt{(c-a)^2 + (d-b)^2}$$

Cartesian coordinate system is used for the drawing of 2-dimentional shapes, and is also commonly used for functions.

Example:

Draw the function   y = (1 - x)/2

To draw a linear function, we need at least 2 points.
If we put that x=0 then value for y would be:

$$y = \frac{1-x}{2} = \frac{1-0}{2} = \frac{1}{2}$$

We found the 1st point, let's name it A, with following coordinates:

A = (0,1/2)

To find the 2nd point, we can put that x=1. Here, the value for y would be:

$$y = \frac{1-x}{2} = \frac{1-1}{2} = \frac{0}{2} = 0$$

If we denote the 2nd point with B, then the coordinates for this point are:

B=(1,0)

Since we have 2 points necessary for the function, we find them in the coordinate system and we connect them with a line that represents the function,

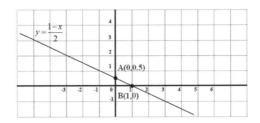

Perimeter Area and Volume

Perimeter and Area (2-dimentional shapes)

Perimeter of a shape determines the length around that shape, while the area includes the space inside the shape.

Rectangle:

$P = 2a + 2b$
$A = ab$

Square

$P = 4a$
$A = a^2$

Parallelogram

$P = 2a + 2b$
$A = ah_a = bh_b$

Rhombus

P = 4a
A = ah = $d_1d_2/2$

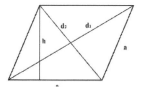

Triangle

P = a + b + c
A = $ah_a/2$ = $bh_b/2$ = $ch_c/2$

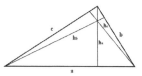

Equilateral Triangle

P = 3a
A = $(a^2\sqrt{3})/4$

Trapezoid

P = a + b + c + d
A = $((a + b)/2)h$

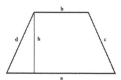

Circle

P = 2r $\prod$
A = r^2 $\prod$

Area and Volume (3-dimentional shapes)

To calculate the area of a 3-dimentional shape, we calculate the areas of all sides and then we add them all.

To find the volume of a 3-dimentional shape, we multiply the area of the base (B) and the height (H) of the 3-dimentional shape.

$$V = BH$$

In case of a pyramid and a cone, the volume would be divided by 3.

$$V = BH/3$$

Here are some of the 3-dimentional shapes with formulas for their area and volume:

Cuboids

A = 2(ab + bc + ac)
V = abc

Cube

$A = 6a^2$
$V = a^3$

Pyramid

$A = ab + ah_a + bh_b$

$V = abH/3$

Cylinder

$A = 2r^2 \prod + 2r\prod H$
$V = r^2\prod H$

Cone

$A = (r + s)r\prod$
$V = (r^2\prod H)/3$

Pythagorean Geometry

If we have a right triangle ABC, where its sides (legs) are a and b and c is a hypotenuse (the side opposite the right angle), then we can establish a relationship between these sides using the following formula:

$c^2 = a^2 + b^2$

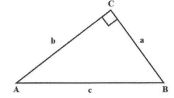

This formula is proven in the Pythagorean Theorem. There are many proofs of this theorem, but we'll look at just one geometrical proof:

If we draw squares on the right triangle's sides, then the area of the square upon the hypotenuse is equal to the sum of the areas of the squares that are upon other two sides of the triangle. Since the areas of these squares are a^2, b^2 and c^2, that is how we got the formula above.

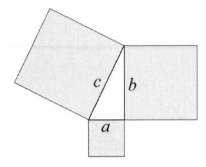

One of the famous right triangles is one with sides 3, 4 and 5. And we can see here that:

$3^2 + 4^2 = 5^2$
$9 + 16 = 25$
$25 = 25$

Example Problem:

The isosceles triangle ABC has a perimeter of 18 centimeters, and the difference between its base and legs is 3 centimeters. Find the height of this triangle.

We write the information we have about triangle ABC and we draw a picture of it for better understanding of the relation

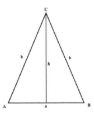

between its elements:

P=18 cm
$a - b = 3$ cm
h=?

We use the formula for the perimeter of the isosceles triangle, since that is what is given to us:

P=a+2b=18 cm

Notice that we have 2 equations with 2 variables, so we can solve it as a system of equations:

a + 2b = 18
a − b = 3 / a + 2b = 18
2a - 2b = 6 / a + 2b + 2a - 2b = 18 + 6
3a = 24
a = 24/3 = 8 cm

Now we go back to find b:
a - b = 3
8 - b = 3
b = 8 - 3
b = 5 cm

Using Pythagorean Theorem, we can find the height using a and b, because the height falls on the side a at the right angle. Notice that height cuts side a exactly in half, and that's why we use in the formula a/2. In this case, b is our hypotenuse, so we have:

$b^2 = (a/2)^2 + h^2$
$h^2 = b^2 - (a/2)^2$
$h^2 = 5^2 - (8/2)^2$
$h^2 = 5^2 - (8/2)^2$
$h^2 = 25 - 4^2$
$h^2 = 26 - 16$
$h^2 = 9$
h = 3 cm.

Quadrilaterals

Quadrilaterals are 2-dimentional geometrical shapes that have 4 sides and 4 angles. There are many types of quadrilaterals, depending on the length of its sides and if they are parallel and also depending on the size of its angles. All quadrilaterals have the following properties:

Sum of all interior angles is 360^0

Sum of all exterior angles is 360^0

A quadrilateral is a parallelogram is it fulfills at least one of the following conditions:

Angles on each side are supplementary
Opposite angles are equal
Opposite sides are equal
Diagonals intersect each other exactly in half

Here are some of the quadrilaterals:

Square

All sides are equal
All angles are right angles

Rectangle

2 pairs of equal sides
All angles are right angles

Parallelogram

2 pairs of equal sides
Opposite angles are equal

Rhombus

All sides are equal
Opposite angles are equal

Trapezoid

One pair of parallel sides

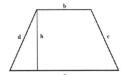

Example Problem

Find all angles of a parallelogram if one angle is greater than the other one by 40^0.

First, we draw an image of a parallelogram:

We denote angles by α and β, Since this is a parallelogram, the opposite angles are equal.

We are given that one angle is greater than the other one by 40^0, so we can write:

β = α + 40^0

We solve this problem in two ways:
1) The sum of all internal angles of every quadrilateral is 360^0. There are 2 α and 2 β. So we have:
2α + 2β = 360^0

Now, instead of β we write α + 40:
2 α + 2 (α + 40^0) = 360^0
2 α + 2 α + 80^0 = 360^0
4 α = 360^0 - 80^0
4 α = 280^0
α = 280^0 / 4
α = 70^0
Now we can find β from α:
β = α + 40^0
β = 70^0 + 40^0
β = 110^0

2) One of the conditions for parallelogram is " Angles on each side are supplementary" and we can use that to find these angles:
α + β = 180^0
α + α + 40^0 = 180^0
2 α = 180^0 - 40^0
2 α = 140^0

α = 70⁰

Now we find β:
β = α + 40⁰
β = 70⁰ + 40⁰
β = 110⁰

Trigonometry

If we are observing a right triangle, where a and b are its legs
and c is its hypotenuse, we can use trigonometric functions
to make a relationship between angles and sides of the right
triangle.

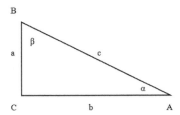

If the right angle of the right triangle ABC is at the point C,
then the sine (sin) and the cosine (cos) of the angles α (at the
point A) and β (at the point B) can be found like this:

$$\sin\alpha = a/c \qquad \sin\beta = b/c$$
$$\cos\alpha = b/c \qquad \cos\beta = a/c$$

Notice that sinα and cosβ are the equal, and same goes for
sinβ and cosα. So, to find sine of the angle, we divide the
side that is opposite of that angle and the hypotenuse. To
find cosine of the angle, we divide the side that makes that
angle (adjacent side) by the hypotenuse.

There are 2 more important trigonometric functions, tangent
and cotangent:

$$tg\alpha = \sin\alpha/\cos\alpha = a/b$$
$$ctg\alpha = \cos\alpha/\sin\alpha = b/a$$

For the functions sine and cosine, there is a table with values for some of the angles, which is to be memorized as it is very useful for solving various trigonometric problems. Here is that table:

	0^0	30^0	45^0	60^0	90^0
$\sin\alpha$	0	1/2	$\sqrt{2}/2$	$\sqrt{3}/2$	1
$\cos\alpha$	1	$\sqrt{3}/2$	$\sqrt{2}/2$	1/2	0

Let's see an example:

If a is 9 cm and c is 18 cm, find α.
We can use the sine for this problem:
$$\sin\alpha = a/c = 9/18 = 1/2$$
We can see from the table that if sinα is 1/2, then angle α is 30^0.

Besides degrees we can write angles using π, where π represents 180^0. For example, angle π/2 means a right angle of 90^0.

Solving inequalities

Basic linear inequalities have one of the following form:

ax + b > 0
ax + b < 0
ax + b ≥ 0
ax + b ≤ 0

where a and b are some real numbers. Our solution to any of these inequalities would be some interval. Let's see one simple example:

2x -10 > 16
2x > 16 + 10

2x > 26

x > 26/2

x > 13

So, the interval here is: (3, +∞)

If we have a case where –x is lesser or greater than some number, then we multiply the whole inequality by -1, where the sign of inequality also changes:

-3x + 9 ≤ 12

-3x ≤ 12 - 9

-3x ≤ 3

-x ≤ 3/-1

x ≤ -3

So, the interval here is: (3, +∞)

Notice the difference in the brackets. This is because this interval contains number 3.

Let's see a little more complex example:

X/(X + 1) > 0

Whenever we have a fraction, we have to make a table:

	-1		0
x	-	-	+
x+1	-	+	+
x/ X + 1	+	-	+

x is positive on the right of the 0, negative on the left of the 0. x+1 is positive on right of the -1, and negative on the left of the -1. If we multiply the signs, we get the signs for the function. We are interested in the positive sign (because we need it to be greater than 0), so the interval is:

$(-\infty, -1) \cup (0, +\infty)$

Logarithms

Logarithm is a function that has the form

$$\log_y x = a$$

It actually solves this equation: which number do we put as a degree on the variable y to get the variable x, that is:

$$y^a = x$$

y is called the base and a is the exponent.

For example, let's solve logarithm $\log_5 25 = a$.

$$5^a = 25$$
$$5^a = 5^2$$
$$a = 2$$

Here, we represent 25 using 5 and the second degree. a and 2 are both on the number 5, so they must be the same.

We can see from the way the logarithm works, that:

$$\log_a 1 = 0 \text{ and } \log_a a = 1$$

From $\log_a 1 = 0$ we have that $a^0 = 1$, which is true for any real number a.

From $\log_a a = 1$ we have that $a^1 = a$, which is true for any real number a.

If in the logarithm the base is 10, then instead of $\log_{10}$ we write l_g.

When we are solving some logarithm, any part can be unknown. In the first example, we had a case where the exponent was the unknown variable. Let's see another example, where both exponent and base are known:

$$l_g x = 2$$
$$10^2 = x$$
$$x = 100$$

Sequences

A sequence of numbers is a set of numbers, but here they are in order. For example, we can represent the set of natural numbers N as a sequence 1, 2, 3,... A sequence can be finite or infinite. In our case of the sequence of the natural numbers, we have an infinite sequence.

If we have a sequence of numbers a_1, a_2, a_3,... we denote that sequence by $\{a_n\}$. We can write, for example, the sequence of natural numbers like this:

$$a_n = a_{n-1} + 1 \quad \text{or} \quad a_{n+1} = a_n + 1$$

From this formula, we can see that each number is greater than the previous number by one, which is true for the sequence of the natural numbers.

The first term (member) of the sequence is denoted by a0. So, if we know the first term of the sequence and we know the formula that describes the sequence, we can find any term of that sequence. Even if we know some other member of the sequence, we can find other members.
Let's solve 2 examples for both cases:

1) If $a_0 = 2$ and $a_n = a_{n-1} - 2$, find the 4th member of the sequence $\{a_n\}$.

Let's find 2nd and 3rd member, which we will use to find the 4th.

$$a_1 = a_0 - 2 = 2 - 2 = 0$$
$$a_2 = a_1 - 2 = 0 - 2 = -2$$
$$a_3 = a_2 - 2 = -2 - 2 = -4$$

So, our 4th member is number -4.

2) If $a_2 = 4$ and $a_n = 2a_{n-1}$, find the 1st member of the sequence $\{a_n\}$.

$$a_2 = 2a_1 \quad \rightarrow \quad 4 = 2a_1 \quad \rightarrow \quad a_1 = 2$$
$$a_1 = 2a_0 \quad \rightarrow \quad 2 = 2a_0 \quad \rightarrow \quad a_0 = 1$$

So, our first member is 1.

Writing Skills

THIS SECTION CONTAINS A SELF-ASSESSMENT AND WRITING SKILLS TU-
TORIALS. The tutorials are designed to familiarize general
principals and the self-assessment contains general
questions similar to the writing skills questions likely to be
on the COMPASS® exam, but are not intended to be identical
to the exam questions. The tutorials are not designed to be a
complete course, and it is assumed that students have some
familiarity with writing skills. If you do not understand parts
of the tutorial, or find the tutorial difficult, it is recommended
that you seek out additional instruction.

Tour of the COMPASS® Writing Skills Content

The COMPASS® writing skills section has 20 questions. Below is a list of the likely writing skills topics likely to appear
on the COMPASS®. Make sure that you understand these
topics at the very minimum.

- English grammar

- English usage

- Punctuation

- Subject - verb agreement

- Sentence structure

The questions in the self-assessment are not the same as
you will find on the COMPASS® - that would be too easy! And

nobody knows what the questions will be and they change all the time. Mostly, the changes consist of substituting new questions for old, but the changes also can be new question formats or styles, changes to the number of questions in each section, changes to the time limits for each section, and combining sections. So, while the format and exact wording of the questions may differ slightly, and changes from year to year, if you can answer the questions below, you will have no problem with the writing skills section of the COMPASS®.

Writing skills Self-Assessment

The purpose of the self-assessment is:

- Identify your strengths and weaknesses.

- Develop your personalized study plan (above)

- Get accustomed to the COMPASS® format

- Extra practice – the self-assessments are almost a full 3rd practice test!

- Provide a baseline score for preparing your study schedule.

Since this is a Self-assessment, and depending on how confident you are with writing skills, timing yourself is optional. The COMPASS® has 20 questions. This self-assessment has 20 questions, so allow about 20 minutes to complete.

Once complete, use the table below to assess your understanding of the content, and prepare your study schedule described in chapter 1.

80% - 100%	Excellent – you have mastered the content
60 – 79%	Good. You have a working knowledge. Even though you can just pass this section, you may want to review the tutorials and do some extra practice to see if you can improve your mark.
40% - 59%	Below Average. You do not understand the content. Review the tutorials , and retake this quiz again in a few days, before proceeding to the practice test questions.
Less than 40%	Poor. You have a very limited understanding. Please review the tutorials , and retake this quiz again in a few days, before proceeding to the practice test questions.

Writing skills Answer Sheet

1. (A) (B) (C) (D) 11. (A) (B) (C) (D) 21. (A) (B) (C) (D)

2. (A) (B) (C) (D) 12. (A) (B) (C) (D) 22. (A) (B) (C) (D)

3. (A) (B) (C) (D) 13. (A) (B) (C) (D) 23. (A) (B) (C) (D)

4. (A) (B) (C) (D) 14. (A) (B) (C) (D) 24. (A) (B) (C) (D)

5. (A) (B) (C) (D) 15. (A) (B) (C) (D) 25. (A) (B) (C) (D)

6. (A) (B) (C) (D) 16. (A) (B) (C) (D)

7. (A) (B) (C) (D) 17. (A) (B) (C) (D)

8. (A) (B) (C) (D) 18. (A) (B) (C) (D)

9. (A) (B) (C) (D) 19. (A) (B) (C) (D)

10. (A) (B) (C) (D) 20. (A) (B) (C) (D)

1. The older children <u>have already eat</u> their dinner, but the baby <u>has not yet ate anything</u>.

   a. The older children have already eat their dinner, but the baby has not yet eaten anything.

   b. The older children have already eaten their dinner, but the baby has not yet ate anything.

   c. The older children have already eaten their dinner, but the baby has not eaten anything yet.

   d. No change is necessary.

2. Its important for you to know <u>it's</u> official name; <u>it's</u> called the Confederate Museum.

   a. Its important for you to know its official name; its called the Confederate Museum.

   b. It's important for you to know it's official name; it's called the Confederate Museum.

   c. It's important for you to know its official name; it's called the Confederate Museum.

   d. No change is necessary.

3. He would have postponed the camping trip, if he <u>would have known</u> about the forecast.

   a. No change is necessary.

   b. If he would have known about the forecast, he would have postponed the camping trip.

   c. If he have known about the forecast, he would have postponed the camping trip.

   d. If he had known about the forecast, he would have postponed the camping trip.

4. He <u>don't have any</u> money to buy clothes and neither do I.

a. He doesn't have any money to buy clothes and neither do I.

b. He doesn't have any money to buy clothes and neither does I.

c. He don't have any money to buy clothes and neither does I.

d. No change is necessary.

5. Because it really doesn't matter, I <u>doesn't care</u> if I go there.

a. Because it really don't matter, I don't care if I go there.

b. Because it really doesn't matter, I don't care if I go there.

c. Because it really don't matter, I don't care if I go there.

d. No change is necessary

6. The mother <u>would not of</u> punished her daughter if could of avoided it.

a. The mother would not of punished her daughter if she could have avoided it.

b. The mother would not have punished her daughter if she could of avoided it.

c. No changes are necessary.

d. The mother would not have punished her daughter if she could have avoided it.

7. There was scarcely <u>no food</u> in the pantry, because <u>not nobody</u> ate at home.

a. There was scarcely no food in the pantry, because nobody ate at home.

b. There was scarcely any food in the pantry, because nobody ate at home.

c. There was scarcely any food in the pantry, because not nobody ate at home.

d. No changes are necessary.

8. Michael <u>has lived</u> in that house for forty years, while I <u>have owned</u> this one for only six weeks.

a. Michael has lived in that house for forty years, while I has owned this one for only six weeks.

b. Michael have lived in that house for forty years, while I have owned this one for only six weeks.

c. Michael have lived in that house for forty years, while I has owned this one for only six weeks.

d. No change is necessary.

9. Lee pronounced <u>its</u> name incorrectly; <u>it's</u> an impatiens, not an impatience.

a. Lee pronounced it's name incorrectly; it's an impatiens, not an impatience.

b. Lee pronounced its name incorrectly; its an impatiens, not an impatience.

c. Lee pronounced it's name incorrectly; its an impatiens, not an impatience.

d. No change is necessary.

10. After the car was fixed it <u>ran good</u> again.

a. No change is necessary.

b. After the car was fixed it ran well again.

c. After the car was fixed it would have run well again.

d. After the car was fixed it ran more well again.

11. Ted and Janice <u>who had been friends for years went on vacation together</u> every summer.

a. Ted and Janice, who had been friends for years, went on vacation together every summer.

b. Ted and Janice who had been friends for years, went on vacation together every summer.

c. Ted, and Janice who had been friends for years, went on vacation together every summer.

d. None of the choices are correct.

12. None of us want to go to the <u>party not even</u> if there will be live music.

a. None of us want to go to the party not even, if there will be live music.

b. None of us want to go to the party, not even if there will be live music.

c. None of us want to go to the party; not even if there will be live music.

d. None of the choice are correct.

13. <u>John, Maurice, and Thomas,</u> quit school two months before graduation.

    a. John, Maurice, and Thomas quit school two months before graduation.

    b. John, Maurice and Thomas quit school two months before graduation.

    c. John Maurice and Thomas, quit school two months before graduation.

    d. None of the choice are correct.

14. "My father said that he would be there on <u>Sunday",</u> <u>Lee</u> explained.

    a. "My father said that he would be there on Sunday" Lee explained.

    b. None of the choices are correct.

    c. "My father said that he would be there on Sunday," Lee explained.

    d. "My father said that he would be there on Sunday." Lee explained.

15. I own two<u> dogs, a cat, named Jeffrey and Henry, the</u> <u>goldfish.</u>

    a. I own two dogs, a cat named Jeffrey, and Henry, the goldfish.

    b. I own two dogs a cat, named Jeffrey, and Henry, the goldfish.

    c. I own two dogs, a cat named Jeffrey; and Henry, the goldfish.

    d. None of the choices are correct.

16. Choose the sentence below with the correct punctuation.

    a. Marcus who won the debate tournament, is the best speaker that I know.

    b. Marcus, who won the debate tournament, is the best speaker that I know.

    c. Marcus who won the debate tournament is the best speaker that I know.

    d. Marcus who won the debate tournament is the best speaker, that I know.

17. The ceremony had an emotional <u>affect</u> on the groom, but the bride was not <u>affected</u>.

    a. The ceremony had an emotional effect on the groom, but the bride was not affected.

    b. The ceremony had an emotional affect on the groom, but the bride was not affected.

    c. The ceremony had an emotional effect on the groom, but the bride was not effected.

18. Anna was taller <u>than Luis, but then</u> he grew four inches in three months.

    a. None of the choices are correct.

    b. Anna was taller then Luis, but than he grew four inches in three months.

    c. Anna was taller than Luis, but than he grew four inches, in three months.

    d. Anna was taller than Luis, but then he grew four inches in three months.

19. There second home is in Boca Raton, but they're not there for most of the year.

> a. Their second home is in Boca Raton, but there not their for most of the year.
>
> b. They're second home is in Boca Raton, but they're not there for most of the year.
>
> c. Their second home is in Boca Raton, but they're not there for most of the year.
>
> d. None of the choices are correct.

20. Their going to graduate in June; after that, their best option will be to go there.

> a. They're going to graduate in June; after that, their best option will be to go there.
>
> b. There going to graduate in June; after that, their best option will be to go there.
>
> c. They're going to graduate in June; after that, there best option will be to go their.
>
> d. None of the choices are correct.

21. Your mistaken; that is not you're book.

> a. You're mistaken; that is not you're book.
>
> b. Your mistaken; that is not your book.
>
> c. You're mistaken; that is not your book.
>
> d. None of the choices are correct.

22. You're classes are on the west side of campus, but you're living on the east side.

   a. You're classes are on the west side of campus, but you're living on the east side.

   b. Your classes are on the west side of campus, but your living on the east side.

   ✓ c. Your classes are on the west side of campus, but you're living on the east side.

   d. None of the choices are correct.

23. The Chinese lives in one of the world's most populous nations, while a citizen of Bermuda lives in one of the least populous.

   – a. The Chinese live in one of the world's most populous nations, while a citizen of Bermuda lives in one of the least populous.

   b. The Chinese lives in one of the world's most populous nations, while a citizen of Bermuda live in one of the least populous.

   c. The Chinese live in one of the world's most populous nations, while a citizen of Bermuda live in one of the least populous.

   d. None of the choices are correct.

24. You shouldn't sit in that chair wearing black pants; I sit the white cat there just a moment ago.

   ✓ a. You shouldn't sit in that chair wearing black pants; I set the white cat there just a moment ago.

   b. You shouldn't set in that chair wearing black pants; I sit the white cat there just a moment ago.

   c. You shouldn't set in that chair wearing black pants; I set the white cat there just a moment ago.

   d. None of the choices are correct.

25. We saw the <u>golden gate Bridge in San Francisco.</u>

    a. Golden Gate Bridge in San Francisco

    b. golden gate bridge in San Francisco

    c. Golden gate bridge in San Francisco

    d. None of the choice are correct.

Answer Key

1. C
Present perfect. You cannot use the Present Perfect with specific time expressions such as: yesterday, one year ago, last week, when I was a child, at that moment, that day, one day, etc. The Present Perfect is used with unspecific expressions such as: ever, never, once, many times, several times, before, so far, already, yet, etc.

2. C
Its vs. It's. "It's" is a contraction for it is or it has. "Its" is a possessive pronoun meaning, more or less, of it or belonging to it.

3. D
The third conditional is used for talking about an unreal situation (that did not happen) in the past. For example, "If I had studied harder, [if clause] I would have passed the exam [main clause]. Which is the same as, "I failed the exam, because I didn't study hard enough."

4. A
Disagreeing with a negative statement uses "neither."

5. C
Doesn't, does not, or does is used with the third person singular--words like he, she, and it. Don't, do not, or do is used for other subjects.

6. D
The third conditional is used for talking about an unreal situation (that did not happen) in the past. For example, "If I had studied harder, [if clause] I would have passed the exam [main clause]. Which is the same as, "I failed the exam, because I didn't study hard enough."

7. B
Double negative sentence. In double negative sentences, one of the negatives is replaced with "any."

8. D
Present perfect. You cannot use the Present Perfect with specific time expressions such as: yesterday, one year ago, last week, when I was a child, at that moment, that day, one day, etc. The Present Perfect is used with unspecific expressions such as: ever, never, once, many times, several times, before, so far, already, yet, etc.

9. D
Its vs. It's. "It's" is a contraction for it is or it has. "Its" is a possessive pronoun meaning, more or less, of it or belonging to it.

10. B
Present tense, "ran well" is correct. "Ran good" is never correct.

11. A
Use a comma to separate phrases.

12. B
Use a comma separates independent clauses. None of us wants to go to the party, not even if there will be live music.

13. B
Don't use a comma before 'and' in a list.

14. C
Commas always go with a quote and the use of said, explained etc.

15. A
This is an example if a comma which appears before 'and,' but is disambiguating. Without the comma, the sentence would be "I own two dogs, a cat named Jeffrey and Henry, the goldfish." This means there is a cat named Jeffrey and Henry, and a goldfish with no name mentioned. The comma appears to show the distinction.

I own two dogs, a cat named Jeffrey, and Henry, the goldfish.

16. B
Comma separate phrases.

17. A
Affect vs. Effect - "Affect" is a verb (action) and "effect" is a noun (thing).

18. D
Than vs. Then – Than is used for comparison, as in, taller than, and then is used for time, as in, but then...

19. C
There vs. their vs. they're. "There" indicates existence as in, "there are." "Their" indicates possession, as in, "their book." "They're" is the contraction form of "they are."

20. A
There vs. their vs. they're. "There" indicates existence as in, "there are." "Their" indicates possession, as in, "their book." "They're" is the contraction form of "they are."

21. C
Your vs. you're. "Your" is the possessive form of you. "You're" is the contraction form of you are.

22. C
Your vs. you're. "Your" is the possessive form of you. "You're" is the contraction form of you are.

23. A
Singular subjects. "The Chinese" is plural, and "a citizen of Bermuda" is singular.

24. A
Sit vs. Set. Set requires an object – something to set down. "Sit" is something that you do, like sit on the chair.

25. A
Always capitalize proper nouns.

Common English Usage Mistakes - A Quick Review

Like some parts of English grammar, usage is definitely going to be on the exam and there isn't any tricky strategies or shortcuts to help you get through this section.
Here is a quick review of common usage mistakes.

1. May and Might

'May' can act as a principal verb, which can express permission or possibility.

Examples:

Lets wait, the meeting may have started.
May I begin now?

'May' can act as an auxiliary verb, which an expresses a purpose or wish

Examples:

May you find favour in the sight of your employer.

May your wishes come true.
People go to school so that they may be educated.

The past tense of may is might.

Examples:

I asked if I might begin

'Might' can be used to signify a weak or slim possibility or polite suggestion.

Examples:

You might find him in his office, but I doubt it.
You might offer to help if you want to.

2. Lie and Lay

The verb lay should always take an object. The three forms of the verb lay are: laid, lay and laid.

The verb lie (recline) should not take any object. The three forms of the verb lie are: lay, lie and lain.

Examples:

Lay on the bed.
The tables were laid by the students.
Let the little kid lie.
The patient lay on the table.

The dog has lain there for 30 minutes.

Note: The verb lie can also mean "to tell a falsehood". This verb can appear in three forms: lied, lie, and lied. This is different from the verb lie (recline) mentioned above.

Examples:

The accused is fond of telling lies.
Did she lie?

3. Would and should

The past tense of shall is 'should', and so "should" generally follows the same principles as "shall."

The past tense of will is "would," and so "would" generally follows the same principles as "will."

The two verbs 'would and should' can be correctly used interchangeably to signify obligation. The two verbs also have some unique uses too. Should is used in three persons to signify obligation.

Examples:

I should go after work.
People should do exercises everyday.
You should be generous.

"Would" is specially used in any of the three persons, to signify willingness, determination and habitual action.
Examples:

They would go for a test run every Saturday.
They would not ignore their duties.
She would try to be punctual.

4. Principle and Auxiliary Verbs

Two principal verbs can be used along with one auxiliary verb as long as the auxiliary verb form suits the two principal verbs.

Examples:

A number of people have been employed and some promoted.

A new tree has been planted and the old has been cut down.

Again note the difference in the verb form.

5. Can and Could

A. Can is used to express capacity or ability.

Examples:

I can complete the assignment today
He can meet up with his target.

B. Can is also used to express permission.

Examples:

Yes, you can begin

In the sentence below, "can" was used to mean the same thing as "may." However, the difference is that the word "can" is used for negative or interrogative sentences, while "may" is used in affirmative sentences to express possibility.

Examples:

They may be correct.   Positive sentence - use may.
Can this statement be correct? A question using "can."
It cannot be correct. Negative sentence using "can."

The past tense of can is could. It can serve as a principal verb when it is used to express its own meaning.

Examples:

In spite of the difficulty of the test, he could still perform well.
"Could" here is used to express ability.

6. Ought

The verb ought should normally be followed by the word to.

Examples:

I *ought to* close shop now.

The verb 'ought' can be used to express:
A. Desirability

You ought to wash your hands before eating.   It is desirable to wash your hands.

B. Probability
She ought to be on her way back by now.   She is probably on her way.

C. Moral obligation or duty
The government ought to protect the oppressed.   It is the government's duty to protect the oppressed.

7. Raise and Rise

Rise
The verb rise means to go up, or to ascend.
The verb rise can appear in three forms, rose, rise, and risen. The verb should not take an object.

Examples:

The bird rose very slowly.
The trees rise above the house.
My aunt has risen in her career.

Raise
The verb raise means to increase, to lift up.
The verb raise can appear in three forms, raised, raise and raised.

Examples:

He raised his hand.
The workers requested a raise.
Do not raise that subject.

8. Past Tense and Past Participle

Pay attention to the proper use these verbs: sing, show, ring, awake, fly, flow, begin, hang and sink.

Mistakes usually occur when using the past participle and past tense of these verbs as they are often mixed up.

Each of these verbs can appear in three forms:

Sing, Sang, Sung.
Show, Showed, Showed/Shown.
Ring, Rang, Rung.
Awake, awoke, awaken
Fly, Flew, Flown.
Flow, Flowed, Flowed.
Begin, Began, Begun.
Hang, Hanged, Hanged (a criminal)
Hang, Hung, Hung (a picture)
Sink, Sank, Sunk.

Examples:

The stranger rang the door bell. (simple past tense)
I have rung the door bell already. (past participle - an action completed in the past)

The stone sank in the river. (simple past tense)
The stone had already sunk. (past participle - an action completed in the past)

The meeting began at 4:00.
The meeting has begun.

9. Shall and Will

When speaking informally, the two can be used interchange-ably. In formal writing, they must be used correctly.

"Will" is used in the second or third person, while "shall" is used in the first person. Both verbs are used to express a time or even in the future.

Examples:

I shall, We shall (First Person)
You will (Second Person)
They will (Third Person)

This principle however reverses when the verbs are to
be used to express threats, determination, command,
willingness, promise or compulsion. In these instances, will
is now used in first person and shall in the second and third
person.

Examples:

I will be there next week, no matter what.
This is a promise, so the first person "I" takes "will."

You shall ensure that the work is completed.
This is a command, so the second person "you" takes "shall."

I will try to make payments as promised.
This is a promise, so the first person "I" takes "will."

They shall have arrived by the end of the day.
This is a determination, so the third person "they" takes
shall.

Note
A. The two verbs, shall and will should not occur twice in the
same sentence when the same future is being referred to

Example:

I shall arrive early if my driver is here on time.

B. Will should not be used in the first person when
questions are being asked

Examples:

Shall I go ?
Shall we go?

Subject Verb Agreement

Verbs in any sentence must agree with the subject of the sentence both in person and number. Problems usually occur when the verb doesn't correspond to the right subject or the verb fails to match the noun close to it.

Unfortunately, there is no easy way around these principals - no tricky strategy or easy rule. You just have to memorize them.

Here is a quick review:

The verb to be, present (past)

Person	Singular	Plural
First	I am (was)	we are (were)
Second	you are (were)	you are (were)
Third	he, she, it is (was)	they are (were)

The verb to have, present (past)

Person	Singular	Plural
First	I have (had)	we have (had)
Second	you have (had)	you have (had)
Third	he, she, it has (had)	they have (had)

Regular verbs, e.g. to walk, present (past)

Person	Singular	Plural

First	I walk (walked)	we walk (walked)
Second	you walk (walked)	you walk (walked)
Third	he, she, it walks (walked)	they work (walked)

1. Every and Each

When nouns are qualified by "every" or "each," they take a singular verb even if they are joined by 'and'

Examples:

Each mother and daughter *was* a given separate test.
Every teacher and student *was* properly welcomed.

2. Plural Nouns

Nouns like measles, tongs, trousers, riches, scissors etc. are all plural.

Examples:

The trousers *are* dirty.
My scissors *have* gone missing.
The tongs *are* on the table.

3. With and As Well

Two subjects linked by "with" or "as well" should have a verb that matches the first subject.

Examples:

The pencil, with the papers and equipment, *is* on the desk.
David as well as Louis is coming.

4. Plural Nouns

The following nouns take a singular verb:

> politics, mathematics, innings, news, advice,
> summons, furniture, information, poetry, machinery,
> vacation, scenery

Examples:

The machinery *is* difficult to assemble
The furniture *has* been delivered
The scenery *was* beautiful

5. Single Entities

A proper noun in plural form that refers to a single entity requires a singular verb. This is a complicated way of saying;
some things appear to be plural, but are really singular, or
some nouns refer to a collection of things but the collection
is really singular.

Examples:

The United Nations Organization *is* the decision maker in
the matter.

Here the "United Nations Organization" is really only one
"thing" or noun, but is made up of many "nations."

The book, "The Seven Virgins" *was* not available in the
library.

Here there is only one book, although the title of the book is
plural.

6. Specific Amounts are always singular

A plural noun that refers to a specific amount or quantity that is considered as a whole (dozen, hundred, score etc) requires a singular verb.

Examples:

60 minutes *is* quite a long time.
Here "60 minutes" is considered a whole, and therefore one item (singular noun).

The first million is the most difficult.

7. Either, Neither and Each are always singular

The verb is always singular when used with: either, each, neither, every one and many.

Examples:

Either of the boys *is* lying.
Each of the employees *has* been well compensated
Many a police officer *has* been found to be courageous
Every one of the teachers *is* responsible

8. Linking with Either, Or, and Neither match the second subject

Two subjects linked by "either," "or,""nor" or "neither" should have a verb that matches the second subject.

Examples:

Neither David nor Paul *will* be coming.
Either Mary or Tina *is* paying.

Note

If one of the subjects linked by "either," "or,""nor" or "neither" is in plural form, then the verb should also be in plural, and the verb should be close to the plural subject.

Examples:

Neither the mother *nor* her kids *have* eaten.
Either Mary *or* her *friends are* paying.

9. Collective Nouns are Plural

Some collective nouns such as poultry, gentry, cattle, vermin etc. are considered plural and require a plural verb.

Examples:

The *poultry are* sick.
The *cattle are* well fed.

Note

Collective nouns involving people can work with both plural and singular verbs.

Examples:

Nigerians are known to be hard working
Europeans live in Africa

10. Nouns that are Singular and Plural

Nouns like deer, sheep, swine, salmon etc. can be singular or plural and require the same verb form.

Examples:

The swine is feeding. (singular)
The swine are feeding. (plural)

The salmon is on the table. (singular)
The salmon are running upstream. (plural)

11. Collective Nouns are Singular

Collective nouns such as Army, Jury, Assembly, Committee, Team etc should carry a singular verb when they subscribe to one idea. If the ideas or views are more than one, then the verb used should be plural.

Examples:

The committee is in agreement in their decision.

The committee were in disagreement in their decision.
The jury has agreed on a verdict.
The jury were unable to agree on a verdict.

12. Subjects links by "and" are plural.

Two subjects linked by "and" always require a plural verb

Examples:

David and John are students.

Note
If the subjects linked by "and" are used as one phrase, or constitute one idea, then the verb must be singular

The color of his socks and shoe is black.
Here "socks and shoe" are two nouns, however the subject is "color" which is singular.

Punctuation - Colons, Semicolons, Hyphens, Dashes, Parentheses and Apostrophes

Within a sentence there are several different types of punctuation marks that can denote a pause. Each of these punctuation marks has different rules when it comes to its structure and usage, so we will look at each one in turn.

Colons

The colon is used primarily to introduce information. It can start lists such as in the sentence, "There were several things Susan had to get at the store: bread, cereal, lettuce and tomatoes." Or a colon can be used to point out specific information, such as in the sentence, "It was only then that the group fully realized what had happened: The Martian invasion had begun."

Note that if the information after the colon is a complete sentence, you capitalize and punctuate it exactly like you would a sentence. If, however, it does not constitute a complete sentence, you don't have to capitalize anything. ("Peering out the window Meredith saw them: zombies.")

Semicolons

Semicolons can be thought of as super commas. They denote a stronger stop than a comma does, but they are still weaker than a period, not quite capable of ending a sentence. Semicolons are primarily used to separate independent clauses that are not being separated by a coordinating conjunction. ("Chris went to the store; he bought chips and salsa.") Semicolons can only do this, however, when the ideas in each clause are related. For instance, the sentence, "It's raining outside; my sister went to the movies," is not a proper usage of the semicolon since those clauses have nothing to do with each other.

Semicolons can also be used in lists provided that one or more element in the list is itself made up of a smaller list.

If you want to write a list of things you plan to bring to a picnic, and those things only include a Frisbee, a chair and some pasta salad, you would not need to use a semicolon. But if you also wanted to bring plastic knives, forks and spoons, you would need to write your sentence like this: "For our picnic I am bringing a Frisbee; a chair; plastic knives, forks and spoons; and some pasta salad."

Using semicolons like this preserves the smaller list that you have in your larger list.

Hyphens

In order to join words together to show that they are linked you use hyphens. The most common use of hyphens is to link together words to show that they are working together in a sentence. ("The well-known actor was eating at the table behind us.") This shows explicitly that you are using "well-known" as a single concept and not as two descriptive words in a list.

Hyphens can also be used to split a word in half if you run out of space writing on one line of a page. This is often seen in newspapers and magazines when text is justified to both sides of a page or a column. For example:

> The massive earthquake caused surpris-
>
> ingly little damage in the affected areas.

However, you can only use a hyphen in this way if you split the word between syllables. Often students think that they can use hyphens to break up words wherever they want; this is wrong. For the word "surprisingly" you

could have a hyphen between "sur" and "prisingly," "surpris" and "ingly, and between "surprising" and "ly," but nowhere else.

Finally, hyphens can be used to add prefixes to words. This

happens a lot in news reports with phrases such as "pro-government troops."

Dashes and Parentheses

Both dashes and parentheses are used to set aside information into parenthetical statements; statements that can be treated as an aside. They do not need to be there for the sentence to make sense, but the information they provide is interesting enough that you feel it should be included. Parentheses are considered stronger than dashes are. (Commas can also be used to separate nonessential information from a sentence, but they are considered to be the weakest of the three.)

As the previous sentence shows, parentheses can surround entire sentences, separating them from the paragraph. Dashes, on the other hand, can separate off the last statement in a sentence. ("Calvin came home and greeted his family for the first time in days—everyone smiled.") Obviously, that last sentence could also be written using a semicolon or as two sentences. The difference is in how you want it to sound to the reader. Should these thoughts be treated as two distinct pieces? Or should everyone smiling at Calvin be part of the main sentence, just separated a bit more strongly—with a slightly longer pause—than a comma could manage?

Apostrophes

There are two primary uses of the apostrophe in English: forming contractions and forming possessive nouns.

Contractions are formed by taking two words and combining them together with an apostrophe replacing the missing letters (do not becomes don't), or by shortening an existing word (cannot becomes can't). Apostrophes can

also make contractions by attaching verbs to nouns or pronouns. ("He's going to the store.")

When making singular nouns possessive the general rule is that you add an 's to the end of singular nouns. (This is Tim's bagel.) When dealing with plural nouns that do not end with the letter –s (such as children), the rule is that you also add an 's to the end of the word. (It was the children's favorite movie.) And when dealing with plural nouns that end with the letter –s, you simply add an apostrophe. (My sisters' favorite game is tag.)

However, and this is an important "however" given the controversy it can cause, when dealing with singular words that end with the letter –s (such as circus), there are two standards for how to make them possessive—each with its own grammar books to back it up.

One standard says that you still add an 's to the end of the word. (This is the circus's biggest tent.) The other says that, since the word ends with an –s, it can only get an apostrophe. (This is the circus' biggest tent.) Some style books, such as the Chicago Manual of Style will go so far as to say that the former option is correct, but to avoid inflaming people's passions on the subject, using the latter is perfectly acceptable. The best thing to do is to find out which style the teacher or editor you are writing for at any given time prefers and conform to it for that person.

Commas

Commas are probably the most commonly used punctuation mark in English. Commas can break the flow of writing to give it a more natural sounding style, and they are the main punctuation mark used to separate ideas. Commas also separate lists, introductory adverbs, introductory prepositional phrases, dates and addresses.

The most rigid way that commas are used is when separating clauses. There are two primary types of clauses in a sentence, independent and subordinate (sometimes called dependent). Independent clauses are clauses that express a complete thought such as, "Tim went to the store." Subordinate clauses, on the other hand, only express partial thoughts that serve to expand upon an independent clause such as, "after the game ended," which you can see is clearly not a complete sentence. (You will learn more about clauses in different lessons.)

The rule for commas with clauses is that a comma must separate the clauses when a subordinate clause comes first in a sentence: "After the game ended, Tim went to the store." But there should not be a comma when a subordinate clause follows an independent clause: "Tim went to the store after the game ended." If you leave the comma out of the first example, you have a run-on sentence. If you add one into the second example, you have a comma-splice error. Also, when you have two independent clauses joined together with a coordinating conjunction, you need to separate them with a comma. "Tim went to the store, and Beth went home."

There are some artistic exceptions to these rules, such as adding a pause for literary effect, but for the most part they are set in stone.

Commas are also used to separate items in a list. This area of English is unfortunately less clear than it should be, with two separate rules depending on what standard you are following. To understand the two different rules, let's pretend you are having a party at your house, and you are making a list of refreshments your friends will want. You may decide to serve three things: 1) pizza 2) chips 3) drinks. There are two different rules governing how you should punctuate this. According to many grammar books, you would write this as, "At the store I will buy pizza, chips, and drinks." This

variation puts a comma after each item in the list. It is the version that the style books used in most college English and history courses will prefer, so it is probably the one you should follow. However, the Associated Press style guide, which is used in college journalism classes and at newspapers and magazines, says the sentence should be written like this: "At the store I will buy pizza, chips and drinks." Here you only use a comma between the first two words, letting the word "and" act as the separator between the last two.

Another important place to use commas is when you have a modifier that describes an element of a sentence, but that does not directly follow the thing it describes. Look at the sentence: "Tim went over to visit Beth, watching the full moon along the way." In this sentence there is no confusion about who is "watching the full moon"; it is Tim, probably as he walks to Beth's house. If you remove the comma, however, you get this: "Tim went over to visit Beth watching the full moon along the way." Now it sounds as though Beth is watching the full moon, and we are forced to wonder what "way" the moon is traveling along.

Commas are also used when adding introductory prepositional phrases and introductory adverbs to sentences. A comma is always needed following an introductory adverb. ("Quickly, Jody ran to the car.") Commas are even necessary when you have an adverb introducing a clause within a sentence, even if the clause not the first clause of the sentence. ("Amanda wanted to go to the movie; however, she knew her homework was more important.")

With introductory prepositional phrases you only add a comma if the phrase (or if a group of introductory phrases) is five or more words long. Thus, the sentence you just read did not have a comma following its introductory prepositional phrase ("With introductory prepositional phrases") because it was only four words. Compare that to this sentence with a five word introductory phrase: "After the ridiculously long class, the friends needed to relax."

The last main way that commas are used in sentences is to separate out information that does not need to be there. For instance, "My cousin Hector, who wore a blue hat at the party, thought you were funny." The fact that Hector wore a blue hat is interesting, but it is not vital to the sentence; it could be removed and not changed the sentence's meaning. For that reason it gets commas around it. Along these lines you should remember that any clause introduced by the word that is considered to provide essential information to the sentence and should not get commas around it. Conversely, any clause starting with the word which is considered nonessential and should not get commas around it.

Quotation Marks

Quotation marks are used in English in a variety of different ways. The most common use of quotation marks is to show quotations either as dialogue or when directly quoting a source in an essay or news article. Fortunately, both of these uses follow the same basic rules.

When you have a quote written as the second part of a sentence, you need to put a comma before the quotation marks and a period inside the quotation marks at the end. (Franklin said, "Let's go to the store.") Conversely, when you have quote as the first part of the sentence with information describing it second, a comma replaces the period at the end of the sentence inside the quotes. ("Let's go to the store," Franklin said.)

If the information in a quote is not a complete sentence you do not need to capitalize it or put commas around it, provided that it is not dialogue. (No one thought the idea of "going to the store" sounded very fun.)

It is important to note that when the last word in a sentence has both a quotation mark and a period attached to it, the period is always inside the quotes. This is the case when you have a complete sentence inside a quote ("Let's go to the store."), and when the last word in a sentence just happens to have quote marks around it (Kerri said I was "mean.") You also need to do the same thing with commas. (Kerri said I was "mean," and it made me feel bad.) However, other punctuation marks such as colons, semicolons and dashes do not follow this rule and should come outside of the quotes. (Kerri said I was "mean"; it made me feel bad.)

When you want to use a quote inside a quote, you use the standard double-quotation marks for the outer quote and single-quotation marks for the inner quote. ("The sign on the door said 'no soliciting,' so we went to the next house.")

Non-period end punctuation marks—exclamation points and question marks—will sometimes go inside the quotation marks and sometimes outside, depending on how much of the sentence they refer to. If the end punctuation refers only to what is in the quote, it goes inside the quotation marks. ("Everyone fleeing the zombie attack screamed, "Run!") However, if the end punctuation refers to the entire sentence, it goes outside of the quotation marks. ("What is "blue cheese"?)

Quotation marks are also used around certain types of titles. To figure out which ones, it helps to look at which titles are not put in quotes as well.

Titles are generally broken down into two categories: large works and small works. Large works are things such as newspapers, magazines, CDs, books and television shows. The defining characteristic of a large work is that it is able to hold small works in it. Small works are the articles inside newspapers and magazines, the songs on a CD, the chapters in a book and the episodes of a television show. It is small works that get quotation marks around them. (Large works, meanwhile, are either underlined or italicized.)

Using quotation marks correctly in a title looks something like this: The two-page article entitled "San Francisco Giants Win World Series" appeared in yesterday's New York Times. The article title is in quotes, and the newspaper title is in italics.

How to Answer English Grammar Multiple Choice - Verb Tense

This tutorial is designed to help you answer English Grammar multiple choice questions as well as a very quick refresher on verb tenses. It is assumed that you have some familiarity with the verb tenses covered here. If you find these questions difficulty or do not understand the tense construction, we recommend you seek out additional instruction.

Tenses Covered

1. Past Progressive
2. Present Perfect
3. Present Perfect Progressive
4. Present Progressive
5. Simple Future
6. Simple Future – "Going to" Form
7. Past Perfect Progressive
8. Future Perfect Progressive
9. Future Perfect
10. Future Progressive
11. Past Perfect

1. The Past Progressive Tense

How to Recognize This Tense

He *was running* very fast when he fell.

They *were drinking* coffee when he arrived.

About the Past Progressive Tense

This tense is used to speak of an action that was in progress in the past when another event occurred.

The action was unfolding at a point in the past.

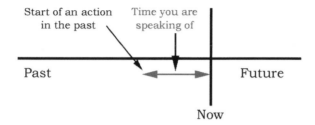

Past Progressive Tense Construction

This tense is formed by using the past tense of the verb "to be" plus the present participle of the main verb.

Sample Question

Bill _____ lunch when we arrived.

     a. will eat

     b. is eating

     c. eats

     d. was eating

How to Answer This Type of Question

1. First examine the question for clues about the time frame.

The sentence ends with "when we arrived," so we know the time frame is a point ("when") in the past (arrived).

The correct answer will refer to an ongoing action at a point of time in the past.

2. Examine the choices and eliminate any obviously incorrect answers.

Choice A is the future tense so we can eliminate.

Choice B is the present continuous so we can eliminate.

Choice C is present tense so we can eliminate.

Choice D refers to an action that takes place at a point of time in the past ("was eating").

2. The Present Perfect Tense

How to Recognize This Tense

I *have had* enough to eat.

We *have been* to Paris many times.

I *have known* him for five years.

I *have been* coming here since I was a child.

About the Present Perfect Tense

This tense expresses the idea that something happened (or didn't happen) at an unspecific time in the past until the present. The action happened at an unspecified time in the past. (If there is a specific time mentioned, the simple past tense is used.) It can be used for repeated action, accomplishments, changes over time and uncompleted action.

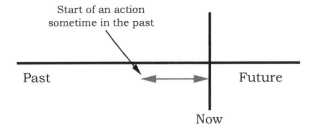

Present Perfect Tense Construction

It is also used with "for" and "since".

This tense is formed by using the present tense of the verb "to have" plus the past participle of the main verb.

Sample Question

I _____ these birds many times.

    a. am seeing

    b. will saw

    c. have seen

    d. have saw

How to Answer This Type of Question

1. First examine the question for clues about the time frame.

"Many times" tells us that the action is repeated and in the past.

2. Examine the choices and eliminate any obviously incorrect answers.

Choice A, "am seeing" is incorrect because it is a continuing action, i.e. in the present; it also doesn't use a form of 'have'.

Choice B is grammatically incorrect.

Choice C is tells of something that has happened in the past and is now over. This is the best choice so far.

Choice D is grammatically incorrect.

3. The Present Perfect Progressive Tense

How to Recognize This Tense

We *have been seeing* a lot of rainy days.

I *have been reading* some very good books.

About the Present Perfect Progressive Tense

This tense expresses the idea that something happened (or didn't happen) in the relatively recent past, but <u>the action is not finished.</u> It is used to express the duration of the action.

NOTE: The present perfect speaks of an action that happened sometime in the past, but this action is finished. In the present perfect progressive tense, the action that started in the past is still going on.

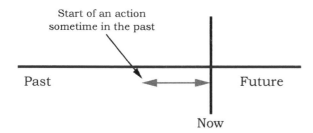

Present Perfect Progressive Tense Construction

This tense is formed by using the present tense of the verb "to have," plus "been," plus the present participle of the main verb.

Sample Question

Bill _____ there for two hours.

    a. sits

    b. sitting

    c. has been sitting

    d. will sat

How to Answer This Type of Question

1. First examine the question for clues about the time frame.

"For two hours" tells us that the action, "sits," is continuous up to now, and may continue into the future.

Note this sentence could also be the simple past tense,

Bill sat there for two hours.

Or the future tense,

Bill will sit there for two hours.

However, these are not among the options.

2. Examine the choices and eliminate any obviously incorrect answers.

Choice A is incorrect because it is the present tense.
Choice B is incorrect because it is the present continuous.
Choice C is correct. "Has been sitting" expresses a continuous action in the past that isn't finished.
Choice D is grammatically incorrect.

4. The Present Progressive Tense

How to Recognize This Tense

We *are having* a delicious lunch.

They *are driving* much too fast.

About the Present Progressive Tense

This tense is used to express what the action is <u>right now</u>. The action started in the recent past, and is continuing into the future.

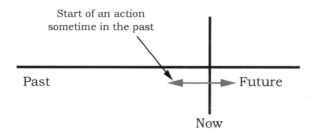

Present Perfect Tense Construction

The Present Progressive Tense is formed by using the present tense of "to be" plus the present participle of the main verb.

Sample Question

She _____ very hard these days.

    a. works

    b. is working

    c. will work

    d. worked

How to Answer This Type of Question

1. First examine the question for clues about the time frame.

The end of the sentence includes "these days" which tell us the action started in the past, continues into the present, and may continue into the future.

2. Examine the choices and eliminate any obviously incorrect answers.

Choice A, the simple present is incorrect.
Choice B, "is working" is correct.
Check the other two choices just to be sure. Choice C is fu-

ture tense, and choice D is past tense, so they can be eliminated.

The correct answer is choice B.

5. The Simple Future Tense

How to Recognize This Tense

I *will see* you tomorrow.
We *will drive* the car.

About the Simple Future Tense

This tense shows that the action will happen some time in the future.

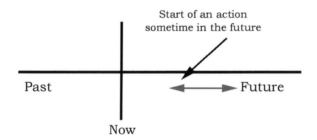

Simple Future Tense Construction

The tense is formed by using "will" plus the root form of the verb. (The root form of the verb is the infinitive without "to." Examples: read, swim.)

Sample Question

We _____ to Paris next year.

    a. went

    b. had been

    c. will go

    d. go

How to Answer This Type of Question

1. First examine the question for clues about the time frame.

The last two words of the sentence, "next year," clearly identify this sentence as referring to the future.

2. Examine the choices and eliminate any obviously incorrect answers.

Choice A is the past tense and can be eliminated.

Choice B is the past perfect tense and can be eliminated.

Choice D is the simple present and can be eliminated.

Choice C is the only one left and is the correct simple future tense.

6. The Simple Future Tense – The "Going to" Form

How to Recognize This Tense

I *am going to* see you tomorrow.

We *are going to* drive the car.

About the Simple Future Tense

This form of the future tense is used to show the intention of doing something in the future. (This is the strict grammatical meaning, but in daily speech, it is often used interchangeably with the simple future tense, the "will" form.)

The tense is formed by using the present conditional tense of "to go," plus the infinitive of the verb.

Sample Question

I _____ shopping in an hour.

    a. go

    b. have gone

    c. am going to go

    d. went

How to Answer This Type of Question

1. First examine the question for clues about the time frame.

"In an hour" clearly identifies the action as taking place in the future.

2. Examine the choices and eliminate any obviously incorrect answers.

Choice A is the simple present tense and can also be eliminated.

Choice B is the past perfect and can be eliminated.

Choice C is the correct answer.

Choice D is the past tense and can be eliminated.

7. The Past Perfect Progressive Tense

How to Recognize This Tense

I *had been sleeping* for an hour when you phoned.

We *had been eating* our dinner when they all came into the dining room.

About the Past Perfect Progressive Tense

This tense is used to show that the action had been going on for a period of time in the past when another action, also in the past, occurred.

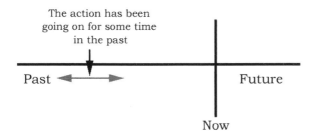

The action has been
going on for some time
in the past

Past

Future

Now

Past Perfect Tense Construction

The tense is formed by using the past perfect tense of the verb "to be" plus the present participle of the main verb.

Sample Question

How long _____ you _____ when I saw you?

    a. are _____ running

    b. had _____ running

    c. had _____ been running

    d. was _____ running

How to Answer This Type of Question

1. First examine the question for clues about the time frame.

"When I saw" tells us the sentence happened at a point of time ("when") in the past ("saw").

2. Examine the choices and eliminate any obviously incorrect answers.

Choice A, "are running" is incorrect and can be eliminated.

Choice B, "Had ___ running" is grammatically incorrect and can be eliminated.

Choice C is correct.

Choice D is grammatically incorrect so the answer is choice C.

8. Future Perfect Progressive Tense

How to Recognize This Tense

I *will have been working* here for two years in March.

I *will have been driving* for four hours when I get there, so I will be tired.

About the Future Perfect Progressive Tense

This tense is used to show that the action continues up to a point of time in the future.

Future Prefect Progressive Tense Construction

This tense is formed by using the future perfect tense of "to be" plus the present participle of the main verb.

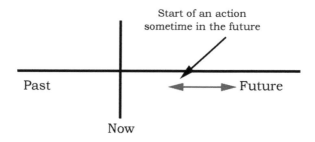

Sample Question

_____ you _____ all the time
I am gone?

    a. have _____ been working

    b. will _____ have been working

    c. are _____ worked

    d. will _____ worked

How to Answer This Type of Question

1. First examine the question for clues about the time frame.

"All the time I am gone" refers to an action in the future ("time I am gone") and the action is progressive ("all the time"). The progressive action means the correct choice will be a verb tense that ends in "ing."

2. Examine the choices and eliminate any obviously incorrect answers.

Choice A, the past perfect, refers to a past continuous event and is also grammatically incorrect in the sentence, so choice A can be eliminated.

Choice B looks correct because it refers to an action will be going on for a period of time in the future.

Examine choices C and D just to be sure. Both choices are grammatically incorrect and can be eliminated. Choice B is the correct answer.

9. The Future Perfect Tense

How to Recognize This Tense

By next November, I *will have received* my promotion.

By the time he gets home, she is going *to have cleaned* the entire house.

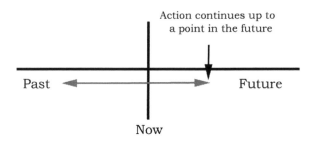

About the Future Perfect Tense

The future perfect tense expresses action in the future before another action in the future. This is the past in the future. For example:

He *will have prepared* dinner when she arrives.

Future Perfect Tense Construction

This tense is formed by "will + have + past participle."

Sample Question

They _____ their seats before the game begins.

    a. will have find

    b. will find

    c. will have found

    d. found

How to Answer This Type of Question

1. First examine the question for clues about the time frame.

This question could be several different tenses. The only clue about the time frame is "before the game begins," which refers to a specific point of time.

We know it isn't in the past, because "begins" is incorrect for the past tense. Similarly with the present. So the question is about something that happens in the future, before another event in the future.

2. Examine the choices and eliminate any obviously incorrect answers.

Choice A can be eliminated as incorrect. Choice B looks good, so mark it and check the others before making a final decision. Choice C is the past perfect and can be eliminated because the time frame is incorrect. Choice D is the simple past tense and can be eliminated for the same reason.

10. Future Progressive Tense

How to Recognize This Tense

The teams *will be playing* soccer when we arrive.

At 3:45 the soccer fans *will be waiting* for the game to start at 4:00 o'clock

At 3:45 the soccer players *will be preparing* to play at 4:00 o'clock

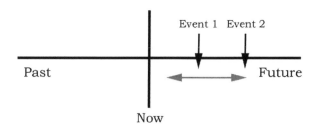

About the Future Progressive Tense

The future progressive tense talks about a continuing action in the future.

Future Progressive Tense Construction

will+ be + (root form) + ing = will be playing

Sample Question

Many excited fans _____ a bus to see the game at 4:00.

    a. catch

    b. catching

    c. have been catching

    d. will be catching

How to Answer This Type of Question

1. First examine the question for clues about the time frame.

"At 4:00," tells us the sentence is either in the past OR in the future.

2. Examine the choices and eliminate any obviously incorrect answers.

From the time frame of the sentence, the answer will be past or future tense.

Choice A is the present tense and can be eliminated. Choice B is the present continuous tense and can be eliminated. Choice C is the past perfect continuous and can be eliminated. Choice D is the only one left. Quickly examining the tense, it is future progressive and is correct in the sentence.

11. The Past Perfect Tense

How to Recognize This Tense

The party *had* just *started* when the coach arrived.

We *had waited* for twenty minutes when the bus finally came.

About the Past Perfect

The past perfect tense talks about two events that happened in the past and establishes which event happened first.

Another example is, "We had eaten when he arrived."

The two events are "eat" and "he arrived." From the sentence above the past perfect tense tells us the first event, "eat" happened before the second event, "he arrived."

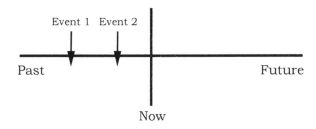

I had already eaten when my friends arrived.

Past Perfect Tense Construction

The past perfect is formed by "have" plus the past participle.

Sample Question

It was time to go home after they _____ the game.

    a. will win

    b. win

    c. had won

    d. wins

How to Answer This Type of Question

1. First examine the question for clues about the time frame.

"Was" tells us the sentence happened in the past. Also notice there are two events, "go home" and "after the game."

2. Examine the choices and eliminate any obviously incorrect answers.

Choice A is the future tense and can be eliminated. Choice B is the simple present and can be eliminated. Choice C is the past perfect and orders the two events in the past. Choice D is the present tense and incorrect and can be eliminated, so choice C is the correct answer.

How to Write an Essay

Writing an essay can be a difficult process, especially if you are under time constraints such as during an exam. Here are three simple steps to help you to write a solid, well thought out essay:

1. **Brainstorm** potential themes and general ideas for your essay.

2. **Outline** your essay step by step, including subheadings for ease of understanding.

3. **Write** your essay carefully being aware of proper grammar and sentence structure.

1. Brainstorming

You should first spend some time thinking about the general subject of the essay. If the essay is asking a question, you must make sure to answer this fully in your essay. You may find it helpful to highlight key words in your assignment or use a simple spider diagram to jot down key ideas.

Example

Read the following information and complete the following assignment:

Joseph Conrad is a Polish author who lived in England for most of his life and wrote a prolific amount of English literature. Much of his work was completed during the height of the British Empire's colonial imperialism.

Assignment: What impact has Joseph Conrad had on modern society? Present your point of view on the matter and support it with evidence. Your evidence may include reasoning, logic, examples from readings, your own experience, and observations.

Joseph Conrad

Background? sailor, adventure, Polish immigrant, Youth, Nostromo, Heart of Darkness
Themes in his works? ivory, silver trading, colonialism, corruption, greed
Thoughts? descent into madness, nature of evil

2. Outlining (or planning)

An outline or plan is critical to organize your thoughts and ideas fully and logically. There are many ways to do this; the easiest is to write down the following headings:

1. Title
2. Introduction
3. Body
4. Conclusion

You should then jot down key ideas and themes that fit logically under the appropriate heading. This plan is now the backbone of your essay.

Tip: Even if you are not required to produce an outline or plan for the assignment, you should always leave it with your essay in the exam booklet or the back of the assignment paper. Simply draw a line across it and write 'plan' or 'outline'. This demonstrates to the reader the approach you use in formulating and finally writing your essay.

3. Writing the essay

Your introduction is what will help the reader to decide whether they want to read the rest of your essay. The introduction also introduces the subject matter and allows you to provide a general background to the reader. The first sentence is very important and you should avoid starting the essay with openers such as 'I will be comparing...'

Example

> Born as Józef Teodor Konrad Korzeniowski on December 3rd, 1857, Joseph Conrad led an adventurous life. As a Polish immigrant, Conrad never quite fit into England where he spent most of his adult life. As a younger man, Conrad made a living off sailing voyages. These swashbuckling experiences soon had him writing tales of the high seas such as one of his first works, Youth. While his early, adventurous work was of high quality, Conrad is best remembered for shedding light on the exploitative side of colonialism. Age and experience led him to start writing about (and challenging) the darker side of the imperial way of thinking. Conrad's work has forever soured words such as colonialism and imperialism.

In the main part, or body of your essay, you should always be yourself and be original.

- Avoid using clichés.
- Be aware of your tone.
- Consider the language that you use. Avoid jargon and slang. Use clear prose and imagery.
- Your writing should always flow; remember to use transitions, especially between paragraphs. Read aloud in your head to make sure a paragraph sounds right.
- Always try to use a new paragraph for new ideas.

Example

> *Conrad's written fiction focused on themes such as greed and power. He portrayed these two concepts as purveyors of evil. Greed and power may take on different guises, but the end result would always be the same.*

Perhaps his most famous piece, The Heart of Darkness, is about the descent of an English ivory trader, Mr. Kurtz, into madness. We are taken up a river resembling the Congo by a narrator, Marlow, who is sent to retrieve Mr. Kurtz. Marlow eventually finds that Kurtz has been diluted by power and greed, the two things that spurred on colonialism in Africa. Kurtz has taken charge of a large tribe of natives (that he brutalizes) and has been hoarding ivory for himself.

Much of Conrad's later work was cut from the same vein as The Heart of Darkness. His crowning achievement is considered Nostromo where he takes an idealistic hero and corrupts him with colonial greed. Only this time the greed is for silver, not ivory.

Conrad's work resonates with readers partly because it was semi-autobiographical. Where his experience sailing the high seas helped bring his adventure stories to light, likewise did his experience witnessing atrocities in Africa reverberate through his writing.

The conclusion is your last chance to impress your reader and brings your entire essay to a logical close. You may want to link your conclusion back to your introduction or provide some closing statements. Do not panic if you cannot close your essay off completely. Few subjects offer closure.

Your conclusion should always be consistent with the rest of the essay and you should never introduce a new idea in your conclusion. It is also important to remember that a weak conclusion can diminish the impact of a good essay.

Example

In sum, Joseph Conrad's life experiences and masterful writing left a lasting impact on the image of progress and what it meant to "move forward". He brought to light the cost in human lives that was required for Europe to continue mining natural resources from foreign lands. Joseph Conrad had a permanent impact on imperial culture, and colonial brutality has been on the decline ever since his work was published.

Presentation

Poor grammar and punctuation can ruin an otherwise good essay. You should always follow any requirements about the presentation of your essay, such as word count. You should also make sure that your writing is legible. Always allow time for one final read-through before submission.

Tip: If you are able to, write with double spacing. If you make a mistake, you can cross it out and write the correction on the blank line above.

Some final points to think about for writing a solid, well thought out essay:

- A good essay will contain a strong focus.

- There is no set essay structure but you can use sub-headings for better readability.

- Avoid particularly sensitive or controversial material. If you must write about something controversial, always make sure to include counter arguments.

- Your essay may have little to do with the subject itself; it is about what you make of the subject.

- Your essay can include examples from your readings, experience, studies or observations.

- Spend time doing practice essays and looking at sample essays beforehand.

Another Example

Lets look at another example using the three steps required to write a good essay:

1. **Brainstorming**

2. **Outlining**

3. **Writing**

Using a second essay, we can now explore these three steps in further detail.

1. Brainstorming

Example

> *Think about the information that follows and the assignment below.*
>
> *People often quote the last two lines of Robert Frost's "The Road not Taken" as being meta-phorical for success. The line's read "I took the one less travelled by, / And that has made all the difference" (19, 20).*
>
> *Assignment: Analyze and interpret this poem. Consider the poem's place in Modernist culture and Robert Frost's personal experiences. Read in between the lines and identify the more complex aspects/themes of this poem. Outline and complete an essay that challenges the point of view presented above, that the poem is synonymous with success. Provide evidence backed up by logic, experience, research, and/ or examples from the poem.*

The assignment and key words that appear in the brief above are being highlighted. This confirms that the essay is not asking a specific question, but rather it is asking for discussion of the subject matter and phrases.
This is the time to take a few moments to jot down initial thoughts about the assignment. Do not worry too much

about proper grammar at this point, just get all your thoughts down on paper:

"The Road Not Taken" by Robert Frost

Background? Modernist poetry
Themes? Life decisions, regret, fate, the unknown future
Thoughts? The diverging roads are symbolic, the sigh at end signifies regret, life has many twists and turns, you can end up in a drastically different situation later after a simple decision now

2. Outlining (or Planning)

Outlining or planning is the next important stage in the process and you should always spend a few minutes writing a plan. This plan is just as important as the essay itself. You can also note how much **time** you may want to spend on a particular section. Make sure to assign headings to each main section of the essay and include important questions/ themes you want to address.

Example

1. Title

2. Essay introduction
Identify and discuss the underlying theme/s in Robert Frost's "The Road Not Taken"
What was Frost's background and its applicability to understanding this poem?

3. Essay body
Quick summary of the poem
Discuss key themes and other concepts
Discuss how these things relate to Modernism

4. Essay conclusion
Rephrase the themes of Robert Frost's poem

and their place in modernist doctrine

This plan is now the outline for the essay.

3. Writing

The introduction is important, as it needs to introduce the reader to the essay in a way that will encourage them to continue reading. A good introduction will introduce the subject matter to a reader and point out relevant information that may be helpful to know when reading the rest of the essay.

Example

> Identify and discuss the underlying theme/s in Robert Frost's "The Road Not Taken"
>
> *Robert Frost wrote during the artistic movement after World War I known as Modernism. One purpose of modernism was to remake things in a new light, to analyze and change symptoms of societies that had plunged the European world into a grisly war. Frost's poem, "The Road Not Taken", carries with it a burden of regret that was a staple of Modernist art.*

This introduction opens with what explaining about the time period of Robert Frost and real life influences to the theme of his poem, "The Road Not Taken". It contains some powerful language that will encourage the reader to continue reading and gives a solid base in understanding the remainder of the essay.

The main part or **body of the essay** is also very important:

Example

> *"The Road Not Taken" was almost assuredly influenced by Robert Frost's personal life. He was very familiar with facing difficult decisions. Frost had to make the decision to send both his sister and daughter to mental institutions. His son Carol committed suicide at the age of 38. The list of loss Frost experienced in*

his life goes on, but it suffices to say he was familiar with questioning the past.

With no other hints of the narrator's identity, it is best to assume that he is a man similar to Frost himself. The poem itself is about a nameless narrator reflecting on when he travelled through the autumn woods one day. He had come across a split in the road and expresses regret that he could not travel both. Each road is described as looking similar and as having equal wear but it is also mentioned one was grassier. The roads were unknown to the narrator, and also shared equal possibilities in how well they may or may not be around their bends.   He tells his listener with a sigh that he had made his decision and had taken "the road less travelled by" (19). Even though he had little idea which road would be better in the long run, the one he chose proved difficult.

This poem is a collection of all the insecurities and possibilities that come with even the simplest decisions. We experience the sorrow expressed by the narrator in the opening lines with every decision we make. For all the choices you make in life, there is a counterweight of choices you have not made. In a way, we are all missing out on half of our lives' possibilities. This realization causes a mixture of regret and nostalgia, but also stokes in us the keen awareness that missed opportunities are inevitable and regretting them is a waste of energy. We often find ourselves stuck, as the narrator is, between questioning the decisions we've made and knowing that this natural process isn't exactly productive.

Unsolvable regret and nostalgia are things that the Modernists fought with on a regular basis. They often experimented in taking happenings of the past and reinventing them to fit a new future.

The body of the essay opens with providing a brief overview of Robert Frost's personal life and his life's relevance to the over arching theme of dealing with difficult decisions in the poem, "The Road Not Taken".

A new paragraph starts where appropriate and at the end of the discussion of Robert Frost's life, a **transition** moves the reader back to the start of the book (closing off this section). This also helps to move the reader towards the next discussion point.

The tone of this essay is formal, mainly because of the seriousness of the subject – regret and nostalgia plays a major role in people's lives all around the world.

For the conclusion, there will be a summary of the main discussion. While it is ideal for you to impress the reader with your writing, more importantly you need to make sure you cover all your bases and address the assignment appropriately with a closing statement about any important points you discussed in the body of your essay.

Example

> *In conclusion, Robert Frost's poem "The Road Not Taken" deals with themes of fate, regret, sorrow, and the many possibilities our decisions hold. Consider how easy it would be to upturn your life today if you made a few decisions you normally wouldn't. Frost's poem forces us to consider the twists and turns our lives take. Perhaps with a sigh, we could all think about the choices that for us have made all the difference.*

This conclusion is consistent with the rest of the essay in terms of style. There are no new ideas introduced and it has referred to the main points in the assignment title.

Finally, a full read-through is necessary before submission. It only takes a couple of minutes to read through and pick up any errors. Remember to double space to leave room for any corrections to be made. You can also leave spacing at the end of each paragraph in case you should need to add an additional sentence or two.

Common Essay Mistakes - Example 1

Whether the topic is love or action, reality television shows damage society. Viewers witness the personal struggles of strangers and they experience an outpouring of emotions in the name of entertainment. This can be dangerous on many levels. Viewers become numb to real emotions and values. Run the risk of not interpreting a dangerous situation correctly. 1 The reality show participant is also at risk because they are completely exposed. 2 The damage to both viewers and participants leads to the destruction of our healthy societal values.

Romance reality shows are dangerous to the participants and contribute to the emotional problems witnessed in society today as we set up a system built on equality and respect, shows like "The Bachelor" tear it down. 3 In front of millions of viewers every week, young women compete for a man. Twenty-five women claim to be in love with a man they just met. The man is reduced to an object they compete for. There are tears, fights, and manipulation aimed at winning the prize. 4 Imagine a young woman's reality when she returns home and faces the scrutiny of viewers who watched her unravel on television every Monday night. These women objectify themselves and have learned 5 that relationships are a combination of hysteria and competition. This does not give hope to a society based on family values and equality.

6 While incorporating the same manipulations and breakdown of relationships offered on "The Bachelor", shows like "Survivor" add another level of danger. Not only are they building a society based on lying to each other, they are competing in physical challenges that become dangerous. In the name of entertainment, these challenges become increasingly physical and are usually held in a hostile environment. The viewer's ability to determine the safety of an activity is messed up. 7 In order to entertain and preserve their pride, participants continue in competitions regardless of the danger level. For example, 8 participants on "Survivor" have sustained serious injuries in the form of heart at-

tack and burns. Societal rules are based on the safety of its
citizens, not on hurting yourself for entertainment.

Reality shows of all kinds are dangerous to participants. They damage society. 9

1. Correct sentence fragments. Who/what runs the risk?
Add a subject or combine sentences. Try: "Viewers become
numb to real emotions and run the risk of not interpreting a
dangerous situation correctly."

2. Correct redundant phrases. Try: "The reality show participant is also at risk because they are exposed."

3. Correct run-on sentences. Decide which thoughts
should be separated. Try: "Romance reality shows are
dangerous to participants and contribute to the emotional
problems of society today. As we support a system built
on equality and respect, shows like "The Bachelor" tear it
down."

4. Vary sentence structure and length. Try: "Twenty-five
women claim to be in love with a man who is reduced to
being the object of competition. There are tears, fights, and
manipulation aimed at winning the prize."

5. Use active voice. Try: These women objectify themselves
and learned that relationships are a combination of hysteria
and competition.

6. Use transitions to tie paragraphs together. Try: Start
the paragraph with, "Action oriented reality shows are
equally as dangerous to the participants."

7. Avoid casual language/slang. Try: "The viewer's ability
to determine the safety of an activity is compromised."

8. Don't address the essay. Avoid phrases like "for example" and "in conclusion". Try: "Participants on "Survivor"
have sustained serious injuries in the form of heart attack
and burns.

9. Leave yourself time to write a strong conclusion! Try:

Designate 3-5 minutes for writing your conclusion.

Common Essay Mistakes - Example 2

Questioning authority makes society stronger. In every aspect our society, there is an authoritative person or group making rules. There is also the group underneath them who are meant to follow. 1 This is true of our country's public schools as well as our federal government. The right to question authority at both of these levels is guaranteed by the United States Declaration of Independence. People are given the ability to question so that authority figures are kept in check 2 and will be forced to listen to the opinions of other people. Questioning authority leads to positive changes in society and preserves what is already working well.

If students never question the authority of a principal's decisions, the best interest of the student body is lost. Good things 3 may not remain in place for the students and no amendment to the rules are sought. Change requires that authority be questioned. An example of this is Silver Head Middle School in Davie, Florida. Last year, the principal felt strongly about enforcing the school's uniform policy. Some students were not bothered by this. 4 Many students felt the policy disregarded their civil rights. A petition voicing student dissatisfaction was signed and presented to the principal. He met with a student representative to discuss the petition. Compromise was reached in the form of a monthly "casual day". The students were able to promote change and peace by questioning authority.

Even at the level of federal government, our country's ultimate authority, the ability to question is the key to the harmony keeping society strong. Most government officials are elected by the public so they have the right to question their authority. 5 If there's a mandate, law, or statement that citizens aren't 6 happy with, they have recourse. Campaigning for or against a political platform and participating in the electoral process give a voice to every opinion. I think elections are very important. 7 Without this questioning and examination of society's laws, the government will represent only the voice of the authority figure. The success of our society is based on the questioning of authority. 8

Society is strengthened by those who question authority. Dialogue is created between people with different visions and change becomes possible. At both the level of public school and of federal government, the positive effects of questioning authority can be witnessed. Whether questioning the decisions of a single principal or the motives of the federal government, it is the willingness of people to question and create change that allows society to grow. A strong society is inspired by many voices, all at different levels. 9 These voices keep society strong.

1. Write concisely. Combine the sentences to improve understanding and cut unnecessary words. Try: "In every aspect of society, there is an authority making rules and a group of people meant to follow them."

2. Avoid slang. Re-word "kept in check". Try: "People are given the ability to question so that authority figures are held accountable and will be forced to listen to the opinions of other people.

2-2. Cut unnecessary words. Try: "People are given the ability to question so that authority figures are held accountable and will listen to other opinions."

3. Use precise language. What are "good things"?Try: "Interesting activities may not remain in place for the students and no amendment to the rules are sought."

Use correct subject-verb agreement. Be careful to identify the correct subject of your sentence. Try: "Interesting activities may not remain in place for the students and no amendment to the rules is sought."

4. Don't add information that doesn't add value to your argument. Cut: "Some students weren't bothered by this."

5. Check for parallel structure. Who has the right to question whose authority? Try: "Having voted them in, the people have the authority to question public officials."

6. Don't use contractions in academic essays. Try: "If there is a mandate, law, or statement that citizens are not happy with, they have recourse."

7. Don't use the pronoun "I" in persuasive essays. Cut opinions. Cut:"I think elections are very important."

8. Use specific examples to prove your argument. Try: Discuss a particular election in depth.

9. Cut redundant sentences. Cut: "A strong society is inspired by many voices, all at different levels."

Writing Concisely

Concise writing is direct and descriptive. The reader follows the writer's thoughts easily. If your writing is concise, a four paragraph essay is acceptable for standardized tests. It's better to write clearly about fewer ideas than to write poorly about many.

This doesn't always mean using fewer words. It means that every word you use is important to the message. Unnecessary or repetitive information dilutes ideas and weakens your writing. The meaning of the word concise comes from the Latin, "to cut up". If it isn't necessary information, don't waste precious testing minutes writing it down.

Being redundant is a quick way to lengthen a sentence or paragraph, but it takes away your power during a timed essay. While many writers use repetition of phrases and key words to make their point, it's important to remove words that don't add value. Redundancy can confuse and lead you away from your subject when you need to write quickly. Be aware that many redundant phrases are part of our daily language and need to be cut from your essay.

For example, "bouquet of flowers" is a redundant phrase as only the word "bouquet" is necessary. Its definition includes flowers. Be especially careful with words you use to stress a point, such as "completely", "totally", and "very".

First of all, I'd like to thank my family.
Revised: First, I'd like to thank my family.
The school *introduced a new* rule.
Revised: The school introduced a rule.

I am *completely full.*
Revised: I am full.

Your glass is *totally empty*!
Revised: Your glass is empty!

Her artwork is *very unique.*
Revised: Her artwork is unique.

Other ways to cut bulk and time include avoiding phrases that have no meaning or power in your essay. Phrases like "in my opinion", "as a matter of fact", and "due to the fact that" are space and time wasters. Also, change passive verbs to active voice.

In my opinion, the paper is well written.
Revised: The paper is well written.

The book *was written* by the best students.
Revised: The best students wrote the book.

The teacher *is listening* to the students.
The teacher listens to the students.

This assigns action to the subject, shortens, and clarifies the sentence. When time is working against you, precise language is on your side.

Not only should you remove redundant phrases, whole sentences without value should be cut too. Replacing general nouns with specific ones is an effective way to accomplish this.

She screamed as the thing came closer. It was a sharp-toothed dog.
Revised: She screamed as the sharp-toothed dog came

closer.

The revised sentence is precise and the paragraph is improved by combining sentences and varying sentence structure. When editing, ask yourself which thoughts should be connected and which need to be separated. Skim each paragraph as you finish writing it and cut as you go.

Leave three to four minutes for final editing. While reading, make a point to pause at every period. This allows you to "hear" sentences the way your reader will, not how you meant them to sound. This will help you find the phrases and sentences that need to be cut or combined. The result is an essay a grader will appreciate.

Avoiding Redundancy

Duplication and verbosity in English is the use of two or more words that clearly mean the same thing, making one of them unnecessary. It is easy to do use redundant expressions or phrases in a conversation where speech is spontaneous, and common in spoken English. In written English, however, redundancy is more serious and harder to ignore. Here are list of redundant phrases to avoid.

1. Suddenly exploded.

An explosion is instantaneous or immediate and that is sudden enough. No need to use 'suddenly' along with exploded.

2. Final outcome.

An outcome refers to the result. An outcome is intrinsically final and so no need to use final along with outcome.

3. Advance notice/planning/reservations/ warning.

A warning, notice, reservation or plan is made before an event. Once the reader sees any of these words, they know that they were done or carried out before the event. These words do not need to be used with advance.

4. First began, new beginning.

Beginning signals the start or the first time, and therefore the use of "new" is superfluous.

5. Add an additional.

The word 'add' indicates the provision of another something, and so "additional" is superfluous.

6. For a period/number of days.

The word "days" is already in plural and clearly signifies more than just one day. It is thus redundant to use "a number of," or "a period of" along with days. Simply state the number of days or of the specific number of days is unknown, you say 'many days.'

7. Foreign imports.

Imports are foreign as they come from another country, so it is superfluous to refer to imports as "foreign."

8. Forever and ever.

Forever indicates eternity and so there is no need for "ever" as it simply duplicated forever.

9. Came at a time when.

"At a time" is not necessary in this phrase because the 'when' already provides a temporal reference to the action, coming.

10. Free gift.

It cannot be a gift if it is paid for. A gift, by nature, is free and so referring to a gift is free is redundant.

11. Collaborate/join/meet/merge together.

The words merge, join, meet and collaborate already suggest people or things coming together. It is unnecessary to use any of these words with together, such as saying merge together or join together. The correct expression is to simply say join or merge, omitting the together.

12. Invited guests.

Guests are those invited for an event. Since they had to be invited to be guests, there is no need to use invited with guests.

13. Major breakthrough.

A breakthrough is significant by nature. It can only be described as a breakthrough when there is a notable progress. The significant nature of the progress is already implied when you use the word "breakthrough," so "major" is redundant.

14. Absolutely certain or sure/essential/ guaranteed.

When someone or something is said to be sure or certain it indicates that it is without doubt. Using "absolutely" in addition to certain or sure is unnecessary. Essential or guaranteed is used for something that is absolute and so also does not need the word absolutely to accompany them.

15. Ask a question.

Ask means to present a question. Using "question" in addition to "ask" is redundant.

16. Basic fundamentals/essentials.

Using basic here is redundant. Essentials and fundamental suggest an elementary nature.

17. [Number] a.m. in the morning/p.m. in the evening.

When you write 8 a.m. the reader knows you mean 8 o'clock in the morning. It is not necessary to say 8 a.m. in the morning. Simply write 8 a.m. or 8 p.m.

18. Definite decision.

A decision is already definite even if it can be reversed later. A decision is a definite course of action has been chosen. No need to use the word definite along with the word decision.

19. Past history/record.

A record or history by definition refers to past events or occurrences. Using past to qualify history or record is unnecessary.

20. Consensus of opinion.

Consensus means agreement over something that may be or not be an opinion. So it may look that using the phrase 'consensus of opinion' is appropriate, but it is better to omit "opinion."

21. Enter in.

Enter means going in, as no one enters out. There fore no need to add "in," simply use "enter."

22. Plan ahead.

You cannot plan for the past. Planning can only be done for the future. When you use "plan," the future is already implied.

23. Possibly might.

The words might and possibly signify probability, so just use one at a time.

24. Direct confrontation.

A confrontation is a head-on conflict, and does not need to be modified with "direct."

25. Postpone until later.

Something postponed is delayed or moved to a later time, and does not need to be modified with "later."

26. False pretense.

The word pretense is only used to describe a deception, so a "false" pretense is redundant.

27. Protest against.

Protest involves showing opposition; there is no need to use against.

28. End result.

Result only comes at the end. The reader who sees the word 'result' already knows that it occurs at the end.

29. Estimated at about/roughly.

Estimates are approximations that are not expected to be accurate, and do not need to be modified with "roughly" or "about."

30. Repeat again.

Repeat refers to something done again and does not need to be modified with "again."

31. Difficult dilemma.

A dilemma is a situation that is complicated or difficult, and does not need to be modified with "difficult."

32. Revert back.

Revert indicates returning to a former or earlier state. Something that reverts goes back to how it used to be. No need to add back.

33. (During the) course (of).

During means "in or throughout the duration of," and doesn't require the use of the word "course."

34. Same identical.

Same and identical means the same thing and should not be used together.

35. Completely filled/finished/opposite.

Completely indicates thoroughness. However, the words finished and filled already indicate something thoroughly filled or finished to the extent possible. The words filled and finished thus do not need to be qualified with "completely."

36. Since the time when.

In this phrase, 'the time when' is not necessary as 'since' already indicates sometime in the past.

37. Close proximity/scrutiny.

Proximity means being close, in respect to location. Scrutiny means studying something closely. Both words already suggest close, whether in respect to location as with proximity, or in respect to study, as with scrutiny. It is therefore unnecessary to use the words together.

38. Spell out in detail.

'Spell out' involves providing details, so no need to add "in detail."

39. Written down.

Anything written can be said to be taken down. Written should therefore be used on its own.

40. (Filled to) capacity.

Anything that is filled has reached its capacity and so the word capacity does not need to be used along with filled.

41. Unintended mistake.

Something is a mistake because it is not intended. The lack of intention is plain and so there is no need to qualify with "unintended."

42. Still remains.

"Remains" signifies that something is still as it is, and so using 'still' is superfluous.

43. Actual experience/fact.

Something becomes an experience after it has occurred. If it didn't occur it is not an experience. A fact can only be a fact when it is sure or confirmed. Both experience and fact thus do not need to be modified with "actual."

44. Therapeutic treatment.

Therapeutic refers to the healing or curing of illness. By nature all medical treatment is therapeutic in that it aims to heal or cure. When speaking of medical treatment, there is thus no need to use therapeutic to qualify treatment.

45. At the present time.

"At present" alone indicates the present time or "at this time." Using "at the present time" is the verbose version. Better to just use "at present."

46. Unexpected surprise.

A surprise is unexpected by nature. The unexpected nature is assumed once the word surprised is read or heard. No need to use unexpected to qualify it.

47. As for example.

"As" indicates the use of an example and so it is redundant to say "an example."

48. Usual custom.

A custom refers to something that is observed or done repeatedly or routinely. The use of 'usual' along with custom is not necessary.

49. Added bonus.

Bonus already indicates something extra, in addition to the ordinary. Using "added" to describe the bonus is not necessary.

50. Few in number.

Something is few because it is small in number. No need to use number with few.

Practice Test Questions Set 1

The questions below are not the same as you will find on the COMPASS® - that would be too easy! And nobody knows what the questions will be and they change all the time. Below are general questions that cover the same subject areas as the COMPASS®. So, while the format and exact wording of the questions may differ slightly, and change from year to year, if you can answer the questions below, you will have no problem with the COMPASS®.

For the best results, take these practice test questions as if it were the real exam. Set aside time when you will not be disturbed, and a location that is quiet and free of distractions. Read the instructions carefully, read each question carefully, and answer to the best of your ability.
Use the bubble answer sheets provided. When you have completed the practice questions, check your answer against the Answer Key and read the explanation provided.

Do not attempt more than one set of practice test questions in one day. After completing the first practice test, wait two or three days before attempting the second set of questions.

Reading Answer Sheet

1. (A) (B) (C) (D)   11. (A) (B) (C) (D)

2. (A) (B) (C) (D)   12. (A) (B) (C) (D)

3. (A) (B) (C) (D)   13. (A) (B) (C) (D)

4. (A) (B) (C) (D)   14. (A) (B) (C) (D)

5. (A) (B) (C) (D)   15. (A) (B) (C) (D)

6. (A) (B) (C) (D)   16. (A) (B) (C) (D)

7. (A) (B) (C) (D)   17. (A) (B) (C) (D)

8. (A) (B) (C) (D)   18. (A) (B) (C) (D)

9. (A) (B) (C) (D)   19. (A) (B) (C) (D)

10. (A) (B) (C) (D)   20. (A) (B) (C) (D)

Mathematics Answer Sheet

1. (A) (B) (C) (D)   21. (A) (B) (C) (D)   41. (A) (B) (C) (D)

2. (A) (B) (C) (D)   22. (A) (B) (C) (D)   42. (A) (B) (C) (D)

3. (A) (B) (C) (D)   23. (A) (B) (C) (D)   43. (A) (B) (C) (D)

4. (A) (B) (C) (D)   24. (A) (B) (C) (D)   44. (A) (B) (C) (D)

5. (A) (B) (C) (D)   25. (A) (B) (C) (D)   45. (A) (B) (C) (D)

6. (A) (B) (C) (D)   26. (A) (B) (C) (D)   46. (A) (B) (C) (D)

7. (A) (B) (C) (D)   27. (A) (B) (C) (D)   47. (A) (B) (C) (D)

8. (A) (B) (C) (D)   28. (A) (B) (C) (D)   48. (A) (B) (C) (D)

9. (A) (B) (C) (D)   29. (A) (B) (C) (D)   49. (A) (B) (C) (D)

10. (A) (B) (C) (D)   30. (A) (B) (C) (D)   50. (A) (B) (C) (D)

11. (A) (B) (C) (D)   31. (A) (B) (C) (D)   51. (A) (B) (C) (D)

12. (A) (B) (C) (D)   32. (A) (B) (C) (D)   52. (A) (B) (C) (D)

13. (A) (B) (C) (D)   33. (A) (B) (C) (D)   53. (A) (B) (C) (D)

14. (A) (B) (C) (D)   34. (A) (B) (C) (D)   54. (A) (B) (C) (D)

15. (A) (B) (C) (D)   35. (A) (B) (C) (D)   55. (A) (B) (C) (D)

16. (A) (B) (C) (D)   36. (A) (B) (C) (D)   56. (A) (B) (C) (D)

17. (A) (B) (C) (D)   37. (A) (B) (C) (D)   57. (A) (B) (C) (D)

18. (A) (B) (C) (D)   38. (A) (B) (C) (D)   58. (A) (B) (C) (D)

19. (A) (B) (C) (D)   39. (A) (B) (C) (D)   59. (A) (B) (C) (D)

20. (A) (B) (C) (D)   40. (A) (B) (C) (D)   60. (A) (B) (C) (D)

Writing Skills Answer Sheet

1. Ⓐ Ⓑ Ⓒ Ⓓ   11. Ⓐ Ⓑ Ⓒ Ⓓ   21. Ⓐ Ⓑ Ⓒ Ⓓ

2. Ⓐ Ⓑ Ⓒ Ⓓ   12. Ⓐ Ⓑ Ⓒ Ⓓ   22. Ⓐ Ⓑ Ⓒ Ⓓ

3. Ⓐ Ⓑ Ⓒ Ⓓ   13. Ⓐ Ⓑ Ⓒ Ⓓ   23. Ⓐ Ⓑ Ⓒ Ⓓ

4. Ⓐ Ⓑ Ⓒ Ⓓ   14. Ⓐ Ⓑ Ⓒ Ⓓ   24. Ⓐ Ⓑ Ⓒ Ⓓ

5. Ⓐ Ⓑ Ⓒ Ⓓ   15. Ⓐ Ⓑ Ⓒ Ⓓ   25. Ⓐ Ⓑ Ⓒ Ⓓ

6. Ⓐ Ⓑ Ⓒ Ⓓ   16. Ⓐ Ⓑ Ⓒ Ⓓ   26. Ⓐ Ⓑ Ⓒ Ⓓ

7. Ⓐ Ⓑ Ⓒ Ⓓ   17. Ⓐ Ⓑ Ⓒ Ⓓ   27. Ⓐ Ⓑ Ⓒ Ⓓ

8. Ⓐ Ⓑ Ⓒ Ⓓ   18. Ⓐ Ⓑ Ⓒ Ⓓ   28. Ⓐ Ⓑ Ⓒ Ⓓ

9. Ⓐ Ⓑ Ⓒ Ⓓ   19. Ⓐ Ⓑ Ⓒ Ⓓ   29. Ⓐ Ⓑ Ⓒ Ⓓ

10. Ⓐ Ⓑ Ⓒ Ⓓ   20. Ⓐ Ⓑ Ⓒ Ⓓ   30. Ⓐ Ⓑ Ⓒ Ⓓ

Part 1 - Reading

Questions 1 – 4 refer to the following passage.

Infectious Diseases

An infectious disease is a clinically evident illness resulting from the presence of pathogenic agents, such as viruses, bacteria, fungi, protozoa, multi-cellular parasites, and unusual proteins known as prions. Infectious pathologies are also called communicable diseases or transmissible diseases, due to their potential of transmission from one person or species to another by a replicating agent (as opposed to a toxin).

Transmission of an infectious disease can occur in many different ways. Physical contact, liquids, food, body fluids, contaminated objects, and airborne inhalation can all transmit infecting agents.

Transmissible diseases that occur through contact with an ill person, or objects touched by them, are especially infective, and are sometimes called contagious diseases. Communicable diseases that require a more specialized route of infection, such as through blood or needle transmission, or sexual transmission, are usually not regarded as contagious.

The term infectivity describes the ability of an organism to enter, survive and multiply in the host, while the infectiousness of a disease indicates the comparative ease with which the disease is transmitted. An infection however, is not synonymous with an infectious disease, as an infection may not cause important clinical symptoms. [3]

1. What can we infer from the first paragraph in this passage?

    a. Sickness from a toxin can be easily transmitted from one person to another.

    b. Sickness from an infectious disease can be easily transmitted from one person to another.

    c. Few sicknesses are transmitted from one person to another.

    d. Infectious diseases are easily treated.

2. What are two other names for infections' pathologies?

    a. Communicable diseases or transmissible diseases

    b. Communicable diseases or terminal diseases

    c. Transmissible diseases or preventable diseases

    d. Communicative diseases or unstable diseases

3. What does infectivity describe?

    a. The inability of an organism to multiply in the host.

    b. The inability of an organism to reproduce.

    c. The ability of an organism to enter, survive and multiply in the host.

    d. The ability of an organism to reproduce in the host.

4. How do we know an infection is not synonymous with an infectious disease?

    a. Because an infectious disease destroys infections with enough time.

    b. Because an infection may not cause clinical symptoms or impair host function.

    c. We do not. The two are synonymous.

    d. Because an infection is too fatal to be an infectious disease.

Questions 5 – 7 refer to the following passage.

Thunderstorms

The first stage of a thunderstorm is the cumulus stage, or developing stage. In this stage, masses of moisture are lifted upwards into the atmosphere. The trigger for this lift can be insulation heating the ground producing thermals, areas where two winds converge, forcing air upwards, or, where winds blow over terrain of increasing elevation. Moisture in the air rapidly cools into liquid drops of water, which appears as cumulus clouds.

As the water vapor condenses into liquid, latent heat is released which warms the air, causing it to become less dense than the surrounding dry air. The warm air rises in an updraft through the process of convection (hence the term convective precipitation). This creates a low-pressure zone beneath the forming thunderstorm. In a typical thunderstorm, about 5×10^8 kg of water vapor is lifted, and the quantity of energy released when this condenses is about equal to the energy used by a city of 100,000 in a month. [4]

5. The cumulus stage of a thunderstorm is the

   a. The last stage of the storm.
   b. The middle stage of the storm formation.
   c. The beginning of the thunderstorm.
   d. The period after the thunderstorm has ended.

6. One of the ways the air is warmed is

   a. Air moving downwards, which creates a high-pressure zone.
   b. Air cooling and becoming less dense, causing it to rise.
   c. Moisture moving downward toward the earth.
   d. Heat created by water vapor condensing into liquid.

7. Identify the correct sequence of events.

a. Warm air rises, water droplets condense, creating more heat, and the air rises further.

b. Warm air rises and cools, water droplets condense, causing low pressure.

c. Warm air rises and collects water vapor, the water vapor condenses as the air rises, which creates heat, and causes the air to rise further.

d. None of the above.

Questions 8 – 10 refer to the following passage.

The US Weather Service

The United States National Weather Service classifies thunderstorms as severe when they reach a predetermined level. Usually, this means the storm is strong enough to inflict wind or hail damage. In most of the United States, a storm is considered severe if winds reach over 50 knots (58 mph or 93 km/h), hail is ¾ inch (2 cm) diameter or larger, or if meteorologists report funnel clouds or tornadoes. In the Central Region of the United States National Weather Service, the hail threshold for a severe thunderstorm is 1 inch (2.5 cm) in diameter. Though a funnel cloud or tornado indicates the presence of a severe thunderstorm, the various meteorological agencies would issue a tornado warning rather than a severe thunderstorm warning here.

Meteorologists in Canada define a severe thunderstorm as either having tornadoes, wind gusts of 90 km/h or greater, hail 2 centimeters in diameter or greater, rainfall more than 50 millimeters in 1 hour, or 75 millimeters in 3 hours.

Severe thunderstorms can develop from any type of thunderstorm. [5]

8. What is the purpose of this passage?

a. Explaining when a thunderstorm turns into a tornado.

b. Explaining who issues storm warnings, and when these warnings should be issued.

c. Explaining when meteorologists consider a thunderstorm severe.

d. None of the above.

9. It is possible to infer from this passage that

a. Different areas and countries have different criteria for determining a severe storm.

b. Thunderstorms can include lightning and tornadoes, as well as violent winds and large hail.

c. If someone spots both a thunderstorm and a tornado, meteorological agencies will immediately issue a severe storm warning.

d. Canada has a much different alert system for severe storms, with criteria that are far less.

10. What would the Central Region of the United States National Weather Service do if hail was 2.7 cm in diameter?

a. Not issue a severe thunderstorm warning.

b. Issue a tornado warning.

c. Issue a severe thunderstorm warning.

d. Sleet must also accompany the hail before the Weather Service will issue a storm warning.

Questions 11 – 13 refer to the following passage.

Clouds

A cloud is a visible mass of droplets or frozen crystals float-ing in the atmosphere above the surface of the Earth or other planetary bodies. Another type of cloud is a mass of material in space, attracted by gravity, called interstellar clouds and nebulae. The branch of meteorology which stud-ies clouds is called nephrology. When we are speaking of Earth clouds, water vapor is usually the condensing sub-stance, which forms small droplets or ice crystal. These crys-tals are typically 0.01 mm in diameter. Dense, deep clouds reflect most light, so they appear white, at least from the top. Cloud droplets scatter light very efficiently, so the farther into a cloud light travels, the weaker it gets. This accounts for the gray or dark appearance at the base of large clouds. Thin clouds may appear to have acquired the color of their environment or background. [6]

11. What are clouds made of?

    a. Water droplets

    b. Ice crystals

    c. Ice crystals and water droplets

    d. Clouds on Earth are made of ice crystals and water droplets

12. The main idea of this passage is

    a. Condensation occurs in clouds, having an intense effect on the weather on the surface of the earth.

    b. Atmospheric gases are responsible for the gray color of clouds just before a severe storm happens.

    c. A cloud is a visible mass of droplets or frozen crys-tals floating in the atmosphere above the surface of the Earth or other planetary body.

    d. Clouds reflect light in varying amounts and degrees, depending on the size and concentration of the water droplets.

13. Why are clouds white on top and grey on the bottom?

a. Because water droplets inside the cloud do not reflect light, it appears white, and the further into the cloud the light travels, the less light is reflected making the bottom appear dark.

b. Because water droplets outside the cloud reflect light, it appears dark, and the further into the cloud the light travels, the more light is reflected making the bottom appear white.

c. Because water droplets inside the cloud reflects light, making it appear white, and the further into the cloud the light travels, the more light is reflected making the bottom appear dark.

d. None of the above.

Questions 14 - 17 refer to the following passage.

Keeping Tropical Fish

Keeping tropical fish at home or in your office used to be very popular. Today, interest has declined, but it remains as rewarding and relaxing a hobby as ever. Ask any tropical fish hobbyist, and you will hear how soothing and relaxing watching colorful fish live their lives in the aquarium. If you are considering keeping tropical fish as pets, here is a list of the basic equipment you will need.

A filter is essential for keeping your aquarium clean and your fish alive and healthy. There are different types and sizes of filters and the right size for you depends on the size of the aquarium and the level of stocking. Generally, you need a filter with a 3 to 5 times turn over rate per hour. This means that the water in the tank should go through the filter about 3 to 5 times per hour.

Most tropical fish do well in water temperatures ranging between 24^0C and 26^0C, though each has its own ideal water temperature. A heater with a thermostat is necessary to regulate the water temperature. Some heaters are submersible and others are not, so check carefully before you buy.

Lights are also necessary, and come in a large variety of types, strengths and sizes. A light source is necessary for plants in the tank to photosynthesize and give the tank a more attractive appearance. Even if you plan on using plastic plants, the fish still require light, although here you can use a lower strength light source.

A hood is necessary to keep dust, dirt and unwanted materials out of the tank. Sometimes the hood can also help prevent evaporation. Another requirement is aquarium gravel. This will help improve the aesthetics of the aquarium and is necessary if you plan on having real plants.

14. What is the general tone of this article?

    a. Formal

    b. Informal

    c. Technical

    d. Opinion

15. Which of the following can not be inferred?

    a. Gravel is good for aquarium plants.

    b. Fewer people have aquariums in their office than at home.

    c. The larger the tank, the larger the filter required.

    d. None of the above.

16. What evidence does the author provide to support their claim that aquarium lights are necessary?

    a. Plants require light.

    b. Fish and plants require light.

    c. The author does not provide evidence for this statement.

    d. Aquarium lights make the aquarium more attractive.

17. Which of the following is an opinion?

a. Filter with a 3 to 5 times turn over rate per hour are required.

b. Aquarium gravel improves the aesthetics of the aquarium.

c. An aquarium hood keeps dust, dirt and unwanted materials out of the tank.

d. Each type of tropical fish has its own ideal water temperature.

Questions 18 - 20 refer to the following passage.

Ways Characters Communicate in Theater

Playwrights give their characters voices in a way that gives depth and added meaning to what happens on stage during their play. There are different types of speech in scripts that allow characters to talk with themselves, with other characters, and even with the audience.

It is very unique to theater that characters may talk "to themselves." When characters do this, the speech they give is called a soliloquy. Soliloquies are usually poetic, introspective, moving, and can tell audience members about the feelings, motivations, or suspicions of an individual character without that character having to reveal them to other characters on stage. "To be or not to be" is a famous soliloquy given by Hamlet as he considers difficult but important themes, such as life and death.

The most common type of communication in plays is when one character is speaking to another or a group of other characters. This is generally called dialogue, but can also be called monologue if one character speaks without being interrupted for a long time. It is not necessarily the most important type of communication, but it is the most common because the plot of the play cannot really progress without it.

Lastly, and most unique to theater (although it has been used somewhat in film) is when a character speaks directly to the audience. This is called an aside, and scripts usually specifically direct actors to do this. Asides are usually comical, an inside joke between the character and the audience, and very short. The actor will usually face the audience when delivering them, even if it's for a moment, so the audience can recognize this move as an aside.

All three of these types of communication are important to the art of theater, and have been perfected by famous playwrights like Shakespeare. Understanding these types of communication can help an audience member grasp what is artful about the script and action of a play.

18. According to the passage, characters in plays communicate to

    a. move the plot forward

    b. show the private thoughts and feelings of one character

    c. make the audience laugh

    d. add beauty and artistry to the play

19. When Hamlet delivers "To be or not to be", he can most likely be described as

    a. solitary

    b. thoughtful

    c. dramatic

    d. hopeless

20. The author uses parentheses to punctuate "although it has been used somewhat in film"

    a. to show that films are less important

    b. instead of using commas so that the sentence is not interrupted

    c. because parenthesis help separate details that are not as important

    d. to show that films are not as artistic

Mathematics

1. Brad has agreed to buy everyone a Coke. Each drink costs $1.89, and there are 5 friends. Estimate Brad's cost.

    a. $7
    b. $8
    c. $10
    d. $12

2. Sarah weighs 25 pounds more than Tony does. If together they weigh 205 pounds, how much does Sarah weigh approximately in kilograms? Assume 1 pound = 0.4535 kilograms.

    a. 41
    b. 48
    c. 50
    d. 52

3. What fraction of $1500 is $75?

    a. 1/14
    b. 3/5
    c. 7/10
    d. 1/20

4. Estimate 16 x 230.

   a. 31,000

   b. 301,000

   c. 3,100

   d. 3,000,000

5. Below is the attendance for a class of 45.

Day	Number of Absent Students
Monday	5
Tuesday	9
Wednesday	4
Thursday	10
Friday	6

What is the average attendance for the week?

   a. 88%

   b. 85%

   c. 81%

   d. 77%

6. John purchased a jacket at a 7% discount. He had a membership which gave him an additional 2% discount on the discounted price. If he paid $425, what is the retail price of the jacket?

   a. $460

   b. $470

   c. $466

   d. $472

7. Estimate 215 x 65.

     a. 1,350

     b. 13,500

     c. 103,500

     d. 3,500

8. 10 x 2 – (7 + 9)

     a. 21

     b. 16

     c. 4

     d. 13

9. 40% of a number is equal to 90. What is the half of the number?

     a. 18

     b. 112.5

     c. 225

     d. 120

10. 1/4 + 3/10 =

     a. 9/10

     b. 11/20

     c. 7/15

     d. 3/40

11. A map uses a scale of 1:2,000   How much distance on the ground is 5.2 inches on the map if the scale is in inches?

     a. 100,400

     b. 10,500

     c. 10,440

     d. 1,400

12. A shop sells an equipment for $545. If 15% of the cost was added to the price as value added tax, what is the actual cost of the equipment?

    a. $490.40

    b. $473.91

    c. $505.00

    d. $503.15

13. What is 0.27 + 0.33 expressed as a fraction?

    a. 3/6

    b. 4/7

    c. 3/5

    d. 2/7

14. 5 men have to share a load weighing 10 kg 550 g equally among themselves. How much will each man have to carry?

    a. 900 g

    b. 1.5 kg

    c. 3 kg

    d. 2 kg 110 g

15. 1/4 + 11/16

    a. 9/16

    b. 1 1/16

    c. 11/16

    d. 15/12

16. A square lawn has an area of 62,500 square meters. What is the cost of building fence around it at a rate of $5.5 per meter?

    a. $4,000

    b. $5,500

    c. $4,500

    d. $5,000

17. A mother is 7 times older than her child. In 25 years, her age will be double that of her child. How old is the mother now?

    a. 35

    b. 33

    c. 30

    d. 25

18. Convert 0.28 to a fraction.

    a. 7/25

    b. 3.25

    c. 8/25

    d. 5/28

19. If a discount of 20% is given for a desk and Mark saves $45, how much did he pay for the desk?

    a. $225

    b. $160

    c. $180

    d. $210

20. In a grade 8 exam, students are asked to divide a number by 3/2, but a student mistakenly multiplied the number by 3/2 and the answer is 5 more than the required one. What was the number?

    a. 4

    b. 5

    c. 6

    d. 8

21. Divide 243 by 3^3

    a. 243

    b. 11

    c. 9

    d. 27

22. Solve the following equation $4(y + 6) = 3y + 30$

    a. $y = 20$

    b. $y = 6$

    c. $y = 30/7$

    d. $y = 30$

23. Divide $x^2 - y^2$ by x - y.

    a. x - y

    b. x + y

    c. xy

    d. y - x

24. Solve for x if, $10^2 \times 100^2 = 1000^x$

    a. x = 2

    b. x = 3

    c. x = -2

    d. x = 0

25. Given polynomials A = -2x⁴ + x² - 3x, B = x⁴ - x³ + 5 and C = x⁴ + 2x³ + 4x + 5, find A + B - C.

a. $x^3 + x^2 + x + 10$

b. $-3x^3 + x^2 - 7x + 10$

c. $-2x^4 - 3x^3 + x^2 - 7x$

d. $-3x^4 + x^3 + 2 - 7x$

26. Solve the inequality: $(x - 6)^2 \geq x^2 + 12$

a. $(2, + \infty)$

b. $(2, + \infty)$

c. $(-\infty, 2)$

d. $(12, + \infty)$

27. $7^5 - 3^5 =$

a. 15,000

b. 16,564

c. 15,800

d. 15,007

28. Divide $x^3 - 3x^2 + 3x - 1$ by x - 1.

a. $x^2 - 1$

b. $x^2 + 1$

c. $x^2 - 2x + 1$

d. $x^2 + 2x + 1$

29. Express 9 x 9 x 9 in exponential form and standard form.

a. $9^3 = 719$

b. $9^3 = 629$

c. $9^3 = 729$

d. $10^3 = 729$

30. Using the factoring method, solve the quadratic equation: $x^2 - 5x - 6 = 0$

   a. -6 and 1

   b. -1 and 6

   c. 1 and 6

   d. -6 and -1

31. Divide 0.524 by 10^3

   a. 0.0524

   b. 0.00052

   c. 0.00524

   d. 524

32. Factor the polynomial $x^3y^3 - x^2y^8$.

   a. $x^2y^3(x - y^5)$

   b. $x^3y^3(1 - y^5)$

   c. $x^2y^2(x - y^6)$

   d. $xy^3(x - y^5)$

33. Find the solution for the following linear equation: $5x/2 = 3x + 24/6$

   a. -1

   b. 0

   c. 1

   d. 2

34. $3^2 \times 3^5$

   a. 3^{17}

   b. 3^5

   c. 4^8

   d. 3^7

35. Solve the system, if a is some real number:

ax + y = 1
x + ay = 1

    a. (1,a)

    b. (1/a + 1, 1)

    c. (1/a = 1, 1/a + 1)

    d. (a, 1/a + 1)

36. Solve $3^5 \div 3^8$

    a. 3^3

    b. 3^5

    c. 3^6

    d. 3^4

37. Solve the linear equation: 3(x + 2) - 2(1 - x) = 4x + 5

    a. -1

    b. 0

    c. 1

    d. 2

38. Simplify the following expression: $3x^a + 6a^x - x^a +$ $(-5a^x) - 2x^a$

    a. $a^x + x^a$

    b. $a^x - x^a$

    c. a^x

    d. x^a

39. Add polynomials -3x² + 2x + 6 and -x² - x - 1.

    a. -2x² + x + 5

    b. -4x² + x + 5

    c. -2x² + 3x + 5

    d. -4x² + 3x + 5

40. 10⁴ is not equal to which of the following?

    a. 100,000

    b. 10 x 10 x 10 x 10

    c. 10² x 10²

    d. 10,000

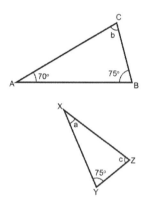

41. What are the respective values of a, b & c if both triangles are similar?

    a. 70°, 70°, 35°

    b. 70°, 35°, 70°

    c. 35°, 35°, 35°

    d. 70°, 35°, 35°

42. For what x is the following equation correct:

$$\log_x 125 = 3$$

a. 1

b. 2

c. 3

d. 5

43. What is the value of the expression $(1 - 4\sin^2(\pi/6))/(1 + 4\cos^2(\pi/3))$?

a. -2

b. -1

c. 0

d. 1/2

44. Calculate $(\sin^2 30^\circ - \sin 0^\circ)/(\cos 90^\circ - \cos 60^\circ)$.

a. -1/2

b. 2/3

c. 0

d. 1/2

45. Consider 2 triangles, ABC and A'B'C', where:

BC = B' C'

AC = A' C'

RA = RA'

Are these 2 triangles congruent?

a. Yes

b. No

c. Not enough information

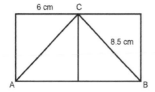

46. What is the perimeter of △ABC in the above shape?

    a. 25.5 cm

    b. 27 cm

    c. 30 cm

    d. 29 cm

47. Find the cotangent of a right angle.

    a. -1

    b. 0

    c. 1/2

    d. -1/2

48. If angle α is equal to the expression 3π/2 - π/6 - π - π/3, find sinα.

    a. 0

    b. 1/2

    c. 1

    d. 3/2

49. Find x if log$_x$(9/25) = 2.

    a. 3/5

    b. 5/3

    c. 6/5

    d. 5/6

50. If $a_0 = 1/2$ and $an=2a_{n-1}{}^2$, find a_2 of the sequence $\{a_n\}$.

   a. 1/2

   b. 1/4

   c. 1/16

   d. 1/24

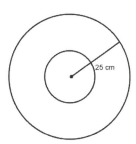

25 cm

51. What is the distance travelled by the wheel above, when it makes 175 revolutions?

   a. 87.5 π m

   b. 875 π m

   c. 8.75 π m

   d. 8750 π m

52. If members of the sequence $\{a_n\}$ are represented by $a_n = (-1)^n a_{n-1}$ and if $a_2 = 2$, find a_0.

   a. 2

   b. 1

   c. 0

   d. -2

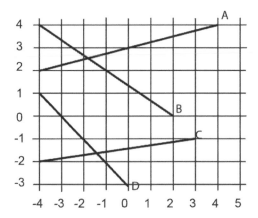

53. Which of the lines above represents the equation 2y – x = 4?

    a. A

    b. B

    c. C

    d. D

54. For any a, find tga/ctga.

    a. -1

    b. 0

    c. 1/2

    d. 1

55. If cosa = 3/5 and b = 24, find side c.

    a. 25

    b. 30

    c. 35

    d. 40

56. Find the sides of a right triangle whose sides are consecutive numbers.

      a. 1, 2, 3

      b. 2, 3, 4

      c. 3, 4, 5

      d. 4, 5, 6

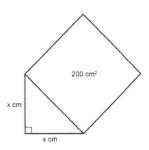

57. What is the length of the sides in the triangle above?

      a. 10

      b. 20

      c. 100

      d. 40

58. Calculate $(\cos(\pi/2) + \operatorname{ctg}(\pi/2))/\sin(\pi/2)$.

      a. -2

      b. -1

      c. 0

      d. 1/2

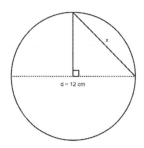

59. Calculate the length of side x.

    a. 6.46

    b. 8.46

    c. 3.6

    d. 6.4

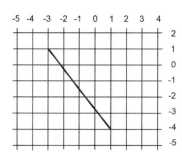

60. What is the slope of the line shown above?

    a. 5/4

    b. -4/5

    c. -5/4

    d. -4/5

Writing Skills

Directions: Select the best option to replace the underlined portion of the sentence.

1. If Joe had told me the truth, <u>I wouldn't have been</u> so angry.

   a. No change is necessary

   b. If Joe would have told me the truth, I wouldn't have been so angry.

   c. I wouldn't have been so angry if Joe would have told the truth.

   d. If Joe would have telled me the truth, I wouldn't have been so angry.

2. Although you may <u>not see nobody in the dark, it does not mean that not nobody</u> is there.

   a. Although you may not see nobody in the dark, it does not mean that nobody is there.

   b. Although you may not see anyone in the dark, it does not mean that not nobody is there.

   c. Although you may not see anyone in the dark, it does not mean that anyone is there.

   d. No change is necessary.

3. The Ford Motor Company was named for Henry Ford, <u>whom</u> had founded the company.

   a. The Ford Motor Company was named for Henry Ford, which had founded the company.

   b. The Ford Motor Company was named for Henry Ford, who founded the company.

   c. The Ford Motor Company was named for Henry Ford, whose had founded the company.

   d. No change is necessary.

4. Thomas Edison <u>will had been known</u> as the greatest inventor since he invented the light bulb, television, motion pictures, and phonograph.

a. Thomas Edison has always been known as the greatest inventor since he invented the light bulb, television, motion pictures, and phonograph.

b. Thomas Edison was always been known as the greatest inventor since he invented the light bulb, television, motion pictures, and phonograph.

c. Thomas Edison must have had been always known as the greatest inventor since he invented the light bulb, television, motion pictures, and phonograph.

d. No change is necessary.

5. The weatherman on Channel 6 said that this has been <u>the hottest summer</u> on record.

a. The weatherman on Channel 6 said that this has been the most hottest summer on record

b. The weatherman on Channel 6 said that this has been the most hottest summer on record

c. The weatherman on Channel 6 said that this has been the hotter summer on record

d. No change is necessary.

6. Although Joe is tall for his age, his brother Elliot is <u>the tallest of the two.</u>

a. Although Joe is tall for his age, his brother Elliot is more tallest of the two.

b. Although Joe is tall for his age, his brother Elliot is the tall of the two.

c. Although Joe is tall for his age, his brother Elliot is the taller of the two.

d. No change is necessary

7. When KISS came to town, all of the tickets <u>was sold out</u> before I could buy one.

a. When KISS came to town, all of the tickets will be sold out before I could buy one.

b. When KISS came to town, all of the tickets had been sold out before I could buy one.

c. When KISS came to town, all of the tickets were being sold out before I could buy one.

d. No change is necessary.

8. The rules of most sports <u>has been</u> more complicated than we often realize.

a. The rules of most sports are more complicated than we often realize.

b. The rules of most sports is more complicated than we often realize.

c. The rules of most sports was more complicated than we often realize.

d. No change is necessary.

9. Neither of the Wright Brothers <u>had any doubts</u> that they would be successful with their flying machine.

a. Neither of the Wright Brothers have any doubts that they would be successful with their flying machine.

b. Neither of the Wright Brothers has any doubts that they would be successful with their flying machine.

c. Neither of the Wright Brothers will have any doubts that they would be successful with their flying machine.

d. No change is necessary.

10. The Titanic <u>has already sunk</u> mere days into its maiden voyage.

  a. The Titanic will already sunk mere days into its maiden voyage.

  b. The Titanic already sank mere days into its maiden voyage.

  c. The Titanic sank mere days into its maiden voyage.

  d. No change is necessary.

11. To make chicken <u>soup; you</u> must first buy a chicken.

  a. To make chicken soup you must first buy a chicken.

  b. To make chicken soup you must first, buy a chicken.

  c. To make chicken soup, you must first buy a chicken.

  d. None of the choices are correct.

12. To travel around <u>the globe you have </u>to drive 25,000 miles.

  a. To travel around the globe, you have to drive 25000 miles.

  b. To travel around the globe, you have to drive, 25000 miles.

  c. None of the choices are correct.

  d. To travel around the globe, you have to drive 25,000 miles.

13. The dog loved chasing <u>bones; but never ate them:</u> it was running that he enjoyed.

  a. The dog loved chasing bones, but never ate them; it was running that he enjoyed.

  b. The dog loved chasing bones; but never ate them, it was running that he enjoyed.

  c. The dog loved chasing bones, but never ate them, it was running that he enjoyed.

  d. None of the choices are correct.

14. <u>However;</u> I believe that he didn't really try that hard.

    a. However, I believe that he didn't really try that hard.

    b. However I believe that he didn't really try that hard.

    c. None of the choices are correct.

    d. However: I believe that he didn't really try that hard.

15. When he's <u>between</u> friends, Robert seems confident, but, <u>between</u> you and me, he is really shy.

    a. None of the choices are correct.

    b. When he's among friends, Robert seems confident, but, among you and me, he is really shy.

    c. When he's between friends, Robert seems confident, but, among you and me, he is really shy.

    d. When he's among friends, Robert seems confident, but, between you and me, he is really shy.

16. I will be finished <u>at about</u> ten in the morning, and will be arriving at home <u>at</u> 6:30.

    a. I will be finished at ten in the morning, and will be arriving at home at about 6:30.

    b. None of the choices are correct.

    c. I will be finished at about ten in the morning, and will be arriving at home at about 6:30.

    d. I will be finished at ten in the morning, and will be arriving at home at 6:30.

17. His home was <u>further</u> than we expected; <u>further</u>, the roads were very bad.

    a. His home was farther than we expected; farther, the roads were very bad.

    b. His home was farther than we expected; further, the roads were very bad.

    c. None of the choices are correct.

    d. His home was further than we expected; farther, the roads were very bad.

18. The man was asked to come with <u>her</u> daughter and <u>his</u> test results.

    a. The man was asked to come with his daughter and her test results.

    b. The man was asked to come with her daughter and her test results.

    c. The man was asked to come with her daughter and our test results.

    d. None of the above.

19. The tables were <u>layed</u> by the students.

    a. The tables were laid by the students.

    b. The tables were lay by the students.

    c. The tables were lie by the students.

    d. None of the choices are correct.

20. Each boy and girl <u>were</u> given a toy.

    a. Each boy and girl were given a toy.

    b. Each boy and girl was given a toy.

    c. A and B are correct.

    d. None of the choices are correct.

21. His measles <u>are</u> getting better.

    a. His measles is getting better.

    b. The sentence is correct.

    c. Both of the choices are correct.

    d. None of the choices are correct.

22. In spite of the bad weather yesterday, he <u>can</u> still attend the party.

    a. The sentence is correct.

    b. In spite of the bad weather yesterday, he could still attend the party.

    c. In spite of the bad weather yesterday, he may still attend the party.

    d. None of the choices are correct.

23. Any girl that fails the test loses <u>her</u> admission.

    a. Any girl that fails the test loses their admission.

    b. Any girl that fails the test loses our admission.

    c. The sentence is correct.

    d. None of the choices are correct.

24. He <u>ought</u> be back by now.

    a. He ought to be back by now.

    b. The sentence is correct.

    c. He ought come back by now.

    d. None of the choices are correct.

25. The man as well as his son <u>have</u> arrived.

    a. The man as well as his son has arrived

    b. The sentence is correct.

    c. None of the choices are correct.

26. Mark and Peter have talked <u>to each other</u>.

    a. The sentence is correct.

    b. Mark and Peter have talked to one another.

    c. None of the choices are correct.

27. Christians believe that their lord <u>have</u> raise.

    a. Christians believe that their lord have raised.

    b. Christians believe that their lord has risen.

    c. The sentence is correct.

    d. None of the choices are correct.

28. Here are the names of people <u>whom</u> you should contact.

    a. The sentence is correct.

    b. Here are the names of people who you should contact

    c. None of the choices are correct.

29. The World Health Organization (WHO) <u>are</u> meeting by January.

    a. The sentence is correct.

    b. The World Health Organization (WHO) is meeting by January.

    c. None of the choices are correct.

30. They <u>shall</u> have to retire when they reach 60 years of age.

    a. They will have to retire when they reach 60 years of age.

    b. The sentence is correct.

    c. None of the choices are correct.

Answer Key

Reading

1. B
We can infer from this passage that sickness from an infectious disease can be easily transmitted from one person to another.

From the passage, "Infectious pathologies are also called communicable diseases or transmissible diseases, due to their potential of transmission from one person or species to another by a replicating agent (as opposed to a toxin)."

2. A
Two other names for infectious pathologies are communicable diseases and transmissible diseases.

From the passage, "Infectious pathologies are also called communicable diseases or transmissible diseases, due to their potential of transmission from one person or species to another by a replicating agent (as opposed to a toxin)."

3. C
Infectivity describes the ability of an organism to enter, survive and multiply in the host. This is taken directly from the passage, and is a definition type question.

Definition type questions can be answered quickly and easily by scanning the passage for the word you are asked to define.

"Infectivity" is an unusual word, so it is quick and easy to scan the passage looking for this word.

4. B
We know an infection is not synonymous with an infectious disease because an infection may not cause important clinical symptoms or impair host function.

5. C
The cumulus stage of a thunderstorm is the beginning of the thunderstorm.

This is taken directly from the passage, "The first stage of a thunderstorm is the cumulus, or developing stage."

6. D
The passage lists four ways that air is heated. One way is, heat created by water vapor condensing into liquid.

7. A
The sequence of events can be taken from these sentences:

As the moisture carried by the [1] air currents rises, it rapidly cools into liquid drops of water, which appear as cumulus clouds. As the water vapor condenses into liquid, it [2] releases heat, which warms the air. This in turn causes the air to become less dense than the surrounding dry air and [3] rise farther.

8. C
The purpose of this text is to explain when meteorologists consider a thunderstorm severe.

The main idea is the first sentence, "The United States National Weather Service classifies thunderstorms as severe when they reach a predetermined level." After the first sentence, the passage explains and elaborates on this idea. Everything is this passage is related to this idea, and there are no other major ideas in this passage that are central to the whole passage.

9. A
From this passage, we can infer that different areas and countries have different criteria for determining a severe storm.

From the passage we can see that most of the US has a criteria of, winds over 50 knots (58 mph or 93 km/h), and hail ¾ inch (2 cm). For the Central US, hail must be 1 inch (2.5 cm) in diameter. In Canada, winds must be 90 km/h or greater, hail 2 centimeters in diameter or greater, and rainfall more than 50 millimeters in 1 hour, or 75 millimeters in 3 hours.

Option D is incorrect because the Canadian system is the same for hail, 2 centimeters in diameter.

10. C
With hail above the minimum size of 2.5 cm. diameter, the Central Region of the United States National Weather Service would issue a severe thunderstorm warning.

11. D
Clouds in space are made of different materials attracted by gravity. Clouds on Earth are made of water droplets or ice crystals.

Choice D is the best answer. Notice also that Choice D is the most specific.

12. C
The main idea is the first sentence of the passage; a cloud is a visible mass of droplets or frozen crystals floating in the atmosphere above the surface of the Earth or other planetary body.

The main idea is very often the first sentence of the paragraph.

13. C
This question asks about the process, and gives options that can be confirmed or eliminated easily.

From the passage, "Dense, deep clouds reflect most light, so they appear white, at least from the top. Cloud droplets scatter light very efficiently, so the farther into a cloud light travels, the weaker it gets. This accounts for the gray or dark appearance at the base of large clouds."

We can eliminate choice A, since water droplets inside the cloud do not reflect light is false.

We can eliminate choice B, since, water droplets outside the cloud reflect light, it appears dark, is false.

Choice C is correct.

14. B
The general tone is informal.

15. B
The statement, " Fewer people have aquariums in their office than at home," cannot be inferred from this article.

16. C
The author does not provide evidence for this statement.

17. B
The following statement is an opinion, " Aquarium gravel improves the aesthetics of the aquarium."

18. D
This question tests the reader's summarization skills. The question is asking very generally about the message of the passage, and the title, "Ways Characters Communicate in Theater", is one indication of that. The other choices A, B, and C are all directly from the text, and therefore readers may be inclined to select one of them, but are too specific to encapsulate the entirety of the passage and its message.

19. B
The paragraph on soliloquies mentions "To be or not to be", and it is from the context of that paragraph that readers may understand that because "To be or not to be" is a soliloquy, Hamlet will be introspective, or thoughtful, while delivering it. It is true that actors deliver soliloquies alone, and may be "solitary" (choice A), but "thoughtful" (choice B) is more true to the overall idea of the paragraph. Readers may choose C because drama and theater can be used interchangeably and the passage mentions that soliloquies are unique to theater (and therefore drama), but this answer is not specific enough to the paragraph in question. Readers may pick up on the theme of life and death and Hamlet's true intentions and select that he is "hopeless" (choice D), but those themes are not discussed either by this paragraph or passage, as a close textual reading and analysis confirms.

20. C
This question tests the reader's grammatical skills. Choice B seems logical, but parenthesis are actually considered to be a stronger break in a sentence than commas are, and along

this line of thinking, actually disrupt the sentence more.

Choices A and D make comparisons between theater and film that are simply not made in the passage, and may or may not be true. This detail does clarify the statement that asides are most unique to theater by adding that it is not completely unique to theater, which may have been why the author didn't chose not to delete it and instead used parentheses to designate the detail's importance (choice C).

Mathematics

1. C
If there are 5 friends and each drink costs $1.89, we can round up to $2 per drink and estimate the total cost at, 5 X $2 = $10.
The actual, cost is 5 X $1.89 = $9.45.

2. D
If we subtract 25 pounds from the total 205, then in remaining 180 pounds, their weights are equal. So Sarah's weight will be = 90 + 25 = 115 pounds.

In kilograms it will be = 115×0.4535 = 52.15 Kg.
Sarah will weigh approximately 52 Kg.

3. D
75/1500 = 15/300 = 3/60 = 1/20

4. C
16 X 230 is about 3,100. The actual number is 3680.

5. B

Day	Number of Absent Students	Number of Present Students	% Attendance
Monday	5	40	88.88%
Tuesday	9	36	80.00%
Wednesday	4	41	91.11%
Thursday	10	35	77.77%
Friday	6	39	86.66%

To find the average or mean, sum the series and divide by the number of items.
88.88 + 80.00 + 91.11 + 77.77 + 86.66/5
424.42/5 = 84.88
Round up to 85%.

Percentage attendance will be 85%

6. C
Let the original price be x, then at the rate of 7% the discounted price will be = 0.93x. 2% discounted amount then will be = 0.02 × 0.93x = 0.0186x. Remaining price = 0.93x - 0.0186x = 0.9114x. This is the amount which John has paid so 0.9114x = 425. X = 425/0.9114. Solving for X = 466.31

7. B
215 X 65 is about 13,500. The exact answer is 13,975.

8. C
10 x 2 − (7 + 9). This is an order of operations question. Do brackets first, then multiplication and division, then addition and subtraction.

10 X 2 - 16

20

9. B
40/100 X = 90
40X = (90 * 100) = 9000
x = 9000/40 = 900/4 = 225

Half of 225 = 112.5

10. B
First, see if you can eliminate any choices. 1/4 + 1/3 is going to equal about 1/2.

Choice A, 9/10 is very close to 1, so it can be eliminated.
Choices B and C are very close to 1/2 so they should be considered.
Choice D is less than half and very close to zero, so it can be eliminated.

Looking at the denominators, Choice C has denominator of 15, and Choice B has denominator of 20. Right away, notice that 20 is common multiple of 4 and 10, and 15 is not.

Confirming - 1/4 + 1/3 = 5/20 + 6/20 = 11/20.

11. C
1 inch on map = 2,000 inches on ground. So 5.2 inches on map = 5.2 x 2,000 = 10,440 inches on ground.

12. B
Actual cost = X, therefore, 545 = x + 0.15x, 545 = 1x + 0.15x, 545 = 1.15x, x = 545/1.15 = 473.9

13. C
0.27 + 0.33 = 0.60 and 0.60 = 60/100 = 3/5

14. D
First convert all units to grams. Since 1000 g = 1 kg, 10 kg = 10 x 1000 = 10,000 + 550 g = 10,550 g. Divide 10,550 among 5 = 10550/5 = 2110 = 2 kg 110 g

15. D
A common denominator is needed, a number which both 4 and 16 will divide into. So, 4+11/16 = 15/16

16. B
As the lawn is square, the length of one side will be the square root of the area. √62,500 = 250 meters. So the perimeters will be 250 × 4 = 1000 meters. The total cost will be 1000 × 5.5 = $5500.

17. A
Suppose the mother's age is x years and the child's is y.
Then $y = 7x$. After 25 years, $y + 25 = 2(x + 25)$. Solving for
y, $y + 25 = 2x + 50$. Putting the value of $y = 7x$ in the below
equation $7x + 25 = 2x + 50$. Solving for $x = 5$ years. So child
is 5 years old and mother is 35.

18. A
$0.28 = 28/100 = 7/25$

19. A
$20/100 = 45/x$
$20x = 4500$
$x = 4500/20 = 450/2 = 225$

20. C
Let the number be x. $(x * 3/2) – (x / 3/2) = 5$
$X = 6$

21. C
$243/3$ x 3 x 3 = $243/27 = 9$

22. B
$4y + 24 = 3y + 30$, $= 4y – 3y + 24 = 30$, $= y + 24 = 30$, $= y =$
$30 – 24$, $= y = 6$

23. B
$(x^2 - y^2) / (x - y) = x + y$

$\underline{-(x^2 - xy)}$
　　$xy - y^2$

$\underline{-(xy - y^2)}$
　　0

24. A
10 x 10 x 100 x 100 = 1000^x, $=100$ x 10,000 = 1000^x, =
1,000,000 = 1000^x = x = 2

25. C
$A + B - C = (-2x^4 + x^2 - 3x) + (x^4 - x^3 + 5) - (x^4 + 2x^3 + 4x + 5)$
$-2x^4 + x^2 - 3x + x^4 - x^3 + 5 - x^4 - 2x^3 - 4x - 5$
$-2x^4 - 3x^3 + x^2 - 7x$

26. C
$(x - 6)^2 \geq x^2 + 12$
$x^2 - 12x + 36 \geq x^2 + 12$
$-12x \geq 12 - 36$
$-12x \geq -24$
$-x \geq -2/-1$
$x \leq 2$

27. B
$(7 \times 7 \times 7 \times 7 \times 7) - (3 \times 3 \times 3 \times 3 \times 3) = 16{,}807 - 243 =$
$16{,}564.$

28. C
$(x^3 - 3x^2 + 3x - 1) / (x - 1) = x^2 - 2x + 1$
$\underline{-(x^3 - x^2)}$
    $-2x^2 + 3x - 1$
  $\underline{-(-2\ x^2 + 2x)}$
         $x - 1$

$\underline{-(x - 1)}$
0

29. C
Exponential form is 9^3 and standard from is 729

30. B
$x^2 - 5x - 6 = 0$
$x^2 - 6x + x - 6 = 0$
$x(x - 6) + x - 6 = 0$
$(x - 6)(x + 1) = 0$
$(x = 6) \cup (x = -1)$

31. B
$0.524/\ 10 \times 10 \times 10 = 0.524/1000 = 0.000524$

32. A
$x^3y^3 - x^2y^8 = x \ *(x^2y^3 - x^2y^3 \ * \ y^5 = x^2y^3(x - y^5)$

33. D
$5x/2 = 3x + 24/6$
$3 * 5x/3 * 2 = 3x + 24/6$
$15x/6 = 3x + 24/6$
$15x = 3x + 24$
$15x - 3x = 25$
$12x = 24$
$x = 24/12 = 2$

34. D
When multiplying exponents with the same base, add the exponents. $3^2 \times 3^5 = 3^{2+5} = 3^7$

35. C
$y = 1 - ax$
$x + a(1 - ax) = 1$
$x + a - a^2x = 1$
$x(1 - a^2) = 1 - a$
$x = 1 - a/1 = a^2 = 1 - a/(1 - a)(1 + a) = 1/a + 1$

$y = 1 - ax$
$y = 1 - a * 1/a + 1 = a/a + 1$
$y = a + 1 - a/a + 1 = 1/a + 1$

36. A
To divide exponents with the same base, subtract the exponents. $3^{8-5} = 3^3$

37. C
$3(x + 2) - 2(1 - x) = 4x + 5$
$3x + 6 - 2 + 2x = 4x + 5$
$5x + 4 = 4x + 5$
$5x - 4x = 5 - 4$
$x = 1$

38. C
$3x^a + 6a^x - x^a + (-5a^x) - 2x^a = 3x^a + 6a^x - x^a - 5a^x - 2x^a = a^x$

39. B
$-4x^2 + x + 5$
$(-3x^2 + 2x + 6) + (-x^2 - x - 1)$
$-3x^2 + 2x + 6 - x^2 - x - 1$
$-4x^2 + x + 5$

40. A
10^4 is not equal to 100,000
$10^4 = 10 \times 10 \times 10 \times 10 = 10^2 \times 10^2 = 10,000$

41. D
Comparing angles on similar triangles, a, b and c will be 70°, 35°, 35°

42. D

$\log_x 125 = 3$
$x^3 = 125$
$x^3 = 5^3$
$x = 5$

43. C

$(1 - 4\sin^2(\pi/6))/(1+4\cos^2(\pi/3)) =$
$(1 - 4\sin^2(30^0))/(1 + 4\cos^2(60^0))$
$(1 - 4(1/2)^2)/(1 + 4(1/2)^2)$
$(1 - 4(1/4))/(1 + 4(1/4))$
$(1 - 1)/(1 + 1) = 0/2 = 0$

44. A

$(\sin^2 30^0 - \sin 0^0)/(\cos 90^0 - \cos 60^0) =$
$((1/2)\ 2 - 0)\ /\ (0-1/2)$
$(1/4)\ /\ (-1/2) = -1/2$

45. A

Yes the triangles are congruent.

46. D

Perimeter of triangle ABC within two squares.
Perimeter = sum of the sides.
Perimeter = 8.5 + 8.5 + 6 + 6
Perimeter = 29 cm.

47. B

$a=90^0$
$\operatorname{ctg}90^0 = \cos 90^0/\sin 90^0 = 0/1 = 0$

48. A

$a = 3\pi/2 - \pi/6 - \pi - \pi/3$
$(9\pi - \pi - 6\pi - 2\pi)/6$
$0\pi/6 = 0$
$\sin a = \sin 0^0 = 0$

49. A

$\log_x(9/25) = 2$
$x^2 = 9/25$
$x^2 = (3/5)^2$
$x = 3/5$

50. A
$a_0 = 1/2$
$a_n = 2a_{n-1}^2$
$a_1 = 2a_0^2 = 2 * (1/2)^2 = 2 * (1/4) = 1/2$
$a_2 = 2a_1^2 = 2 * (1/2)^2 = 2 * (1/4) = 1/2$

51. A
Diameter = 2 x radius.
Circumference = π x Diameter

Distance(meters) = (Circumference x Revolutions)/100
Distance(meters) = [((25 x 2) π) x 175]/100
Distance(meters) = 8750 π/100
Distance = 87.5 π meters.

52. D
$a_n = (-1)^n a_{n-1}$
$a_2 = 2$
$2 = a_2 = (-1)^2 a_1 = a_1 \rightarrow a_1 = 2$
$a_1 = (-1)^1 a_0$
$2 = -a_0$
$a_0 = -2$

53. A
Line A represents the equation $2y - x = 4$.

54. D
$tga/ctga = (sina/cosa)/(cosa/sina) = 1$
or
$tga/ctga = (a/b)/(b/a) = ab/ab = 1$

55. D
$cosa = 3/5 = b/c$
$b = 24$
$3/5 = b/c$
$3/5 = 24/c$
$3c = 5 * 24$
$c = 40$

56. C
The length of the sides is, 3, 4, 5.
x
$y = x + 1$
$z = x + 2$

$x^2 + y^2 = y^2$
$x^2 + (x + 1)^2 = (x + 2)^2$
$x^2 + x^2 + 2x + 1 = x^2 + 4x + 4$
$x^2 - 2x - 3 \ 0$

$x_{1,2} = 2 \pm \sqrt{4} + 12 \ / \ 2$
$x_{1,2} = 2 \pm 4 \ / \ 2$

$x = 3$
$y = 4$
$z = 5$

57. A
Pythagorean Theorem:
$(Hypotenuse)^2 = (Perpendicular)^2 + (Base)^2$
$h^2 = a^2 + b^2$

Given: $h^2 = 200$, $a = b = x$
Then, $x^2 + x^2 = 200$, $2x^2 = 200$, $x^2 = 100$
$x = 10$

58. C
$(\cos(\pi/2) + ctg(\pi/2))/\sin(\pi/2) = (\cos 90^0 + ctg 90^0)/\sin 90^0 = (0+0)/1 = 0$

59. B
Pythagorean Theorem:
$(Hypotenuse)^2 = (Perpendicular)^2 + (Base)^2$
$h^2 = a^2 + b^2$

Given: d (diameter)= 12 & r (radius) = a = b = 6
$h^2 = a^2 + b^2$
$h^2 = 6^2 + 6^2$, $h^2 = 36 + 36$
$h^2 = 72$
$h = 8.46$

60. C
Slope (m) = $\dfrac{\text{change in y}}{\text{change in x}}$

$(x_1, y_1)=(-3,1)$ & $(x_2, y_2)= (1,-4)$
Slope = $[-4 - 1]/[1-(-3)]= -5/4$

Writing Skills

1. A
The third conditional is used for talking about an unreal situation (that did not happen) in the past. For example, "If I had studied harder, [if clause] I would have passed the exam [main clause]. Which is the same as, "I failed the exam, because I didn't study hard enough."

2. C
Double negative sentence. In double negative sentences, one of the negatives is replaced with "any."

3. B
The sentence refers to a person, so "who" is the only correct option.

4. A
The sentence requires the past perfect "has always been known." Furthermore, this is the only grammatically correct choice.

5. B
The superlative, "hottest," is used when expressing a temperature greater than that of anything to which it is being compared.

6. D
When comparing two items, use "the taller." When comparing more than two items, use "the tallest."

7. B
The past perfect form is used to describe an event that occurred in the past and before another event.

8. A
The subject is "rules" so the present tense plural form, "are," is used to agree with "realize."

9. C
The simple past tense, "had," is correct because it refers to completed action in the past.

10. C
The simple past tense, "sank," is correct because it refers to completed action in the past.

11. C
Comma separate phrases.

12. D
The comma separates clauses and numbers are separated with a comma. The correct sentence is,
'To travel around the globe, you have to drive 25,000 miles.'

13. A
The dog loved chasing bones, but never ate them; it was running that he enjoyed.

14. A
When using 'however,' place a comma before and after, except when however begins the sentence.

15. D
Among vs. Between. 'Among' is for more than 2 items, and 'between' is only for 2 items.

When he's among friends (many or more than 2), Robert seems confident, but, between you and me (two), he is very shy.

16. D
At vs. About. At refers to a specific time and about refers to a more general time. A common usage is 'at about 10,' but it isn't proper grammar.

17. B
Further vs. Farther. 'Farther' is used for physical distance, and 'further' is used for figurative distance.

18. A
A Pronoun should conform to its antecedent in gender, number and person.

19. A
The verb "lay" should always take an object. Here the subject is the table. The three forms of the verb lay are: lay, laid

and laid. The sentence above is in past tense.

20. B
Use the singular verb form when nouns are qualified with "every" or "each," even if they are joined by 'and. '

21. B
The sentence is correct. Use a plural verb for nouns like measles, tongs, trousers, riches, scissors etc.

22. B
Use "could," the past tense of "can" to express ability or capacity.

23. C
The sentence is correct. Words such as neither, each, many, either, every, everyone, everybody and any should take a singular pronoun.

24. A
The verb "ought" can be used to express desirability, duty and probability. The verb is usually followed by "to."

25. A
When two subjects are linked with "with" or "as well," use the verb form that matches the first subject.

26. A
When you use 'each other' it should be used for two things or people. When you use 'one another' it should be used for things and people above two

27. B
The verb rise ('to go up', 'to ascend.') can appear in three forms, rise, rose, and risen. The verb should not take an object.

28. A
The sentence is correct. Use "whom" in the objective case, and use "who" a subjective case.

29. B
Use a singular verb with a proper noun in plural form that refers to a single entity. Here the The World Health Organization is a single entity, although it is made up on many members.

30. A

Will is used in the second or third person (they, he, she and you), while shall is used in the first person (I and we). Both verbs are used to express futurity.

Practice Test Questions Set 2

The questions below are not the same as you will find on the COMPASS® - that would be too easy! And nobody knows what the questions will be and they change all the time. Below are general questions that cover the same subject areas as the COMPASS®. So, while the format and exact wording of the questions may differ slightly, and change from year to year, if you can answer the questions below, you will have no problem with the COMPASS®.

For the best results, take these practice test questions as if it were the real exam. Set aside time when you will not be disturbed, and a location that is quiet and free of distractions. Read the instructions carefully, read each question carefully, and answer to the best of your ability.
Use the bubble answer sheets provided. When you have completed the Practice Questions, check your answer against the Answer Key and read the explanation provided.

Do not attempt more than one set of practice test questions in one day. After completing the first practice test, wait two or three days before attempting the second set of questions.

Reading Answer Sheet

1. (A) (B) (C) (D)   11. (A) (B) (C) (D)

2. (A) (B) (C) (D)   12. (A) (B) (C) (D)

3. (A) (B) (C) (D)   13. (A) (B) (C) (D)

4. (A) (B) (C) (D)   14. (A) (B) (C) (D)

5. (A) (B) (C) (D)   15. (A) (B) (C) (D)

6. (A) (B) (C) (D)   16. (A) (B) (C) (D)

7. (A) (B) (C) (D)   17. (A) (B) (C) (D)

8. (A) (B) (C) (D)   18. (A) (B) (C) (D)

9. (A) (B) (C) (D)   19. (A) (B) (C) (D)

10. (A) (B) (C) (D)   20. (A) (B) (C) (D)

Mathematics Answer Sheet

1. (A) (B) (C) (D)   21. (A) (B) (C) (D)   41. (A) (B) (C) (D)

2. (A) (B) (C) (D)   22. (A) (B) (C) (D)   42. (A) (B) (C) (D)

3. (A) (B) (C) (D)   23. (A) (B) (C) (D)   43. (A) (B) (C) (D)

4. (A) (B) (C) (D)   24. (A) (B) (C) (D)   44. (A) (B) (C) (D)

5. (A) (B) (C) (D)   25. (A) (B) (C) (D)   45. (A) (B) (C) (D)

6. (A) (B) (C) (D)   26. (A) (B) (C) (D)   46. (A) (B) (C) (D)

7. (A) (B) (C) (D)   27. (A) (B) (C) (D)   47. (A) (B) (C) (D)

8. (A) (B) (C) (D)   28. (A) (B) (C) (D)   48. (A) (B) (C) (D)

9. (A) (B) (C) (D)   29. (A) (B) (C) (D)   49. (A) (B) (C) (D)

10. (A) (B) (C) (D)   30. (A) (B) (C) (D)   50. (A) (B) (C) (D)

11. (A) (B) (C) (D)   31. (A) (B) (C) (D)   51. (A) (B) (C) (D)

12. (A) (B) (C) (D)   32. (A) (B) (C) (D)   52. (A) (B) (C) (D)

13. (A) (B) (C) (D)   33. (A) (B) (C) (D)   53. (A) (B) (C) (D)

14. (A) (B) (C) (D)   34. (A) (B) (C) (D)   54. (A) (B) (C) (D)

15. (A) (B) (C) (D)   35. (A) (B) (C) (D)   55. (A) (B) (C) (D)

16. (A) (B) (C) (D)   36. (A) (B) (C) (D)   56. (A) (B) (C) (D)

17. (A) (B) (C) (D)   37. (A) (B) (C) (D)   57. (A) (B) (C) (D)

18. (A) (B) (C) (D)   38. (A) (B) (C) (D)   58. (A) (B) (C) (D)

19. (A) (B) (C) (D)   39. (A) (B) (C) (D)   59. (A) (B) (C) (D)

20. (A) (B) (C) (D)   40. (A) (B) (C) (D)   60. (A) (B) (C) (D)

Writing Skills Answer Sheet

1. (A) (B) (C) (D)   11. (A) (B) (C) (D)   21. (A) (B) (C) (D)

2. (A) (B) (C) (D)   12. (A) (B) (C) (D)   22. (A) (B) (C) (D)

3. (A) (B) (C) (D)   13. (A) (B) (C) (D)   23. (A) (B) (C) (D)

4. (A) (B) (C) (D)   14. (A) (B) (C) (D)   24. (A) (B) (C) (D)

5. (A) (B) (C) (D)   15. (A) (B) (C) (D)   25. (A) (B) (C) (D)

6. (A) (B) (C) (D)   16. (A) (B) (C) (D)   26. (A) (B) (C) (D)

7. (A) (B) (C) (D)   17. (A) (B) (C) (D)   27. (A) (B) (C) (D)

8. (A) (B) (C) (D)   18. (A) (B) (C) (D)   28. (A) (B) (C) (D)

9. (A) (B) (C) (D)   19. (A) (B) (C) (D)   29. (A) (B) (C) (D)

10. (A) (B) (C) (D)   20. (A) (B) (C) (D)   30. (A) (B) (C) (D)

Part 1 – Reading and Language Arts

Questions 1 - 4 refer to the following passage.

The Respiratory System

The respiratory system's function is to allow oxygen exchange through all parts of the body. The anatomy or structure of the exchange system, and the uses of the exchanged gases, varies depending on the organism. In humans and other mammals, for example, the anatomical features of the respiratory system include airways, lungs, and the respiratory muscles. Molecules of oxygen and carbon dioxide are passively exchanged, by diffusion, between the gaseous external environment and the blood. This exchange process occurs in the alveolar region of the lungs.

Other animals, such as insects, have respiratory systems with very simple anatomical features, and in amphibians even the skin plays a vital role in gas exchange. Plants also have respiratory systems but the direction of gas exchange can be opposite to that of animals.

The respiratory system can also be divided into physiological, or functional, zones. These include the conducting zone (the region for gas transport from the outside atmosphere to just above the alveoli), the transitional zone, and the respiratory zone (the alveolar region where gas exchange occurs). [8]

1. What can we infer from the first paragraph in this passage?

a. Human and mammal respiratory systems are the same.

b. The lungs are an important part of the respiratory system.

c. The respiratory system varies in different mammals.

d. Oxygen and carbon dioxide are passive exchanged by the respiratory system.

2. What is the process by which molecules of oxygen and carbon dioxide are passively exchanged?

    a. Transfusion

    b. Affusion

    c. Diffusion

    d. Respiratory confusion

3. What organ plays an important role in gas exchange in amphibians?

    a. The skin

    b. The lungs

    c. The gills

    d. The mouth

4. What are the three physiological zones of the respiratory system?

    a. Conducting, transitional, respiratory zones

    b. Redacting, transitional, circulatory zones

    c. Conducting, circulatory, inhibiting zones

    d. Transitional, inhibiting, conducting zones

Questions 5 - 8 refer to the following passage.

Lightning

Lightning is an electrical discharge that occurs in a thunderstorm. Often you'll see it as a bright "bolt" (or streak) coming from the sky. Lightning occurs when static electricity inside clouds builds up and causes an electrical charge. What causes the static electricity? Water! Specifically, water droplets collide with ice crystals after the temperature in the cloud falls below freezing. Sometimes these collisions are small, but other times they're quite large. Large collisions cause large electrical charges, and when they're large enough, look out! The hyper-charged cloud will emit a burst of lightning. This lightning looks quite impressive. For a good reason, too: A lightning bolt's temperature gets so hot that it's sometimes five times hotter than the sun's surface. Although the lightning bolt is hot, it's also short-lived. Because of that, when a person is unfortunate enough to be struck by lightning, their odds of surviving are pretty good. Statistics show that 90% of victims survive a lightning blast. Oh, and that old saying, "Lightning never strikes twice in the same spot"? It's a myth! Many people report surviving lightning blasts three or more times. What's more, lightning strikes some skyscrapers multiple times. The other prominent feature of lightning storms is the thunder. This is caused by the super-heated air around a lightning bolt expands at the speed of sound. We hear thunder after seeing the lightning bolt because sound travels slower than the speed of light. In reality, though, both occur at the same moment.

5. What can we infer from this passage?

 a. An electrical discharge in the clouds causes lightning.

 b. Lightning is not as hot as the temperature of the sun's surface.

 c. The sound that lightning makes occurs when electricity strikes an object.

 d. We hear lightning before we see it.

6. Being struck by lightning means:

 a. Instant death.

 b. Less than a fifty percent chance of survival.

 c. A ninety percent chance of surviving the strike.

 d. An eighty percent chance of survival.

7. Lightning is caused by the following:

 a. Water droplets colliding with ice crystals creating static electricity.

 b. Friction from the clouds rubbing together.

 c. Water droplets colliding.

 d. Warm and cold air mixing together.

Questions 9 - 12 refer to the following passage.

Low Blood Sugar

As the name suggest, low blood sugar is low sugar levels in the bloodstream. This can occur when you have not eaten properly and undertake strenuous activity, or, when you are very hungry. When Low blood sugar occurs regularly and is ongoing, it is a medical condition called hypoglycemia. This condition can occur in diabetics and in healthy adults.

Causes of low blood sugar can include excessive alcohol consumption, metabolic problems, stomach surgery, pancreas, liver or kidneys problems, as well as a side-effect of some medications.

Symptoms

There are different symptoms depending on the severity of the case.

Mild hypoglycemia can lead to feelings of nausea and hunger. The patient may also feel nervous, jittery and have fast heart beats. Sweaty skin, clammy and cold skin are likely symptoms.

Moderate hypoglycemia can result in a short temper, confusion, nervousness, fear and blurring of vision. The patient may feel weak and unsteady.

Severe cases of hypoglycemia can lead to seizures, coma, fainting spells, nightmares, headaches, excessive sweats and severe tiredness.

Diagnosis of low blood sugar

A doctor can diagnosis this medical condition by asking the patient questions and testing blood and urine samples. Home testing kits are available for patients to monitor blood sugar levels. It is important to see a qualified doctor though. The doctor can administer tests to ensure that will safely rule out other medical conditions that could affect blood sugar levels.

Treatment

Quick treatments include drinking or eating foods and drinks with high sugar contents. Good examples include soda, fruit juice, hard candy and raisins. Glucose energy tablets can also help. Doctors may also recommend medications and well as changes in diet and exercise routine to treat chronic low blood sugar.

9. Based on the article, which of the following is true?

    a. Low blood sugar can happen to anyone.

    b. Low blood sugar only happens to diabetics.

    c. Low blood sugar can occur even.

    d. None of the statements are true.

10. Which of the following are the author's opinion?

    a. Quick treatments include drinking or eating foods and drinks with high sugar contents.

    b. None of the statements are opinions.

    c. This condition can occur in diabetics and also in healthy adults.

    d. There are different symptoms depending on the severity of the case

11. What is the author's purpose?

    a. To inform

    b. To persuade

    c. To entertain

    d. To analyze

12. Which of the following is not a detail?

a. A doctor can diagnosis this medical condition by asking the patient questions and testing.

b. A doctor will test blood and urine samples.

c. Glucose energy tablets can also help.

d. Home test kits monitor blood sugar levels.

Questions 13 - 16 refer to the following passage.

Myths, Legend and Folklore

Cultural historians draw a distinction between myth, legend and folktale simply as a way to group traditional stories. However, in many cultures, drawing a sharp line between myths and legends is not that simple. Instead of dividing their traditional stories into myths, legends, and folktales, some cultures divide them into two categories. The first category roughly corresponds to folktales, and the second is one that combines myths and legends. Similarly, we can not always separate myths from folktales. One society might consider a story true, making it a myth. Another society may believe the story is fiction, which makes it a folktale. In fact, when a myth loses its status as part of a religious system, it often takes on traits more typical of folktales, with its formerly divine characters now appearing as human heroes, giants, or fairies. Myth, legend, and folktale are only a few of the categories of traditional stories. Other categories include anecdotes and some kinds of jokes. Traditional stories, in turn, are only one category within the much larger category of folklore, which also includes items such as gestures, costumes, and music. [9]

13. The main idea of this passage is

a. Myths, fables, and folktales are not the same thing, and each describes a specific type of story

b. Traditional stories can be categorized in different ways by different people

c. Cultures use myths for religious purposes, and when this is no longer true, the people forget and discard these myths

d. Myths can never become folk tales, because one is true, and the other is false

14. The terms myth and legend are

a. Categories that are synonymous with true and false

b. Categories that group traditional stories according to certain characteristics

c. Interchangeable, because both terms mean a story that is passed down from generation to generation

d. Meant to distinguish between a story that involves a hero and a cultural message and a story meant only to entertain

15. Traditional story categories not only include myths and legends, but

a. Can also include gestures, since some cultures passed these down before the written and spoken word

b. In addition, folklore refers to stories involving fables and fairy tales

c. These story categories can also include folk music and traditional dress

d. Traditional stories themselves are a part of the larger category of folklore, which may also include costumes, gestures, and music

16. This passage shows that

a. There is a distinct difference between a myth and a legend, although both are folktales

b. Myths are folktales, but folktales are not myths

c. Myths, legends, and folktales play an important part in tradition and the past, and are a rich and colorful part of history

d. Most cultures consider myths to be true

Questions 17 - 19 refer to the following passage.

How To Get A Good Nights Sleep

Sleep is just as essential for healthy living as water, air and food. Sleep allows the body to rest and replenish depleted energy levels. Sometimes we may for various reasons experience difficulty sleeping which has a serious effect on our health. Those who have prolonged sleeping problems are facing a serious medical condition and should see a qualified doctor when possible for help. Here is simple guide that can help you sleep better at night.

Try to create a natural pattern of waking up and sleeping around the same time everyday. This means avoiding going to bed too early and oversleeping past your usual wake up time. Going to bed and getting up at radically different times everyday confuses your body clock. Try to establish a natural rhythm as much as you can.

Exercises and a bit of physical activity can help you sleep better at night. If you are having problem sleeping, try to be as active as you can during the day. If you are tired from physical activity, falling asleep is a natural and easy process for your body. If you remain inactive during the day, you will find it harder to sleep properly at night. Try walking, jogging, swimming or simple stretches as you get close to your bed time.

Afternoon naps are great to refresh you during the day, but

they may also keep you awake at night. If you feel sleepy during the day, get up, take a walk and get busy to keep from sleeping. Stretching is a good way to increase blood flow to the brain and keep you alert so that you don't sleep during the day. This will help you sleep better night.

A warm bath or a glass of milk in the evening can help your body relax and prepare for sleep. A cold bath will wake you up and keep you up for several hours. Also avoid eating too late before bed.

17. How would you describe this sentence?

a. A recommendation

b. An opinion

c. A fact

d. A diagnosis

18. Which of the following is an alternative title for this article?

a. Exercise and a good night's sleep

b. Benefits of a good night's sleep

c. Tips for a good night's sleep

d. Lack of sleep is a serious medical condition

19. Which of the following can not be inferred from this article?

a. Biking is helpful for getting a good night's sleep

b. Mental activity is helpful for getting a good night's sleep

c. Eating bedtime snacks is not recommended

d. Getting up at the same time is helpful for a good night's sleep

Questions 19 - 20 refer to the following passage.

Navy SEAL

The United States Navy's Sea, Air and Land Teams, commonly known as Navy SEALs, are the U.S. Navy's principal special operations force and a part of the Naval Special Warfare Command (NSWC) as well as the maritime component of the United States Special Operations Command (USSOCOM).

The unit's acronym ("SEAL") comes from their capacity to operate at sea, in the air, and on land – but it is their ability to work underwater that separates SEALs from most other military units in the world. Navy SEALs are trained and have been deployed in a wide variety of missions, including direct action and special reconnaissance operations, unconventional warfare, foreign internal defense, hostage rescue, counter-terrorism and other missions. All SEALs are members of either the United States Navy or the United States Coast Guard.

In the early morning of 2 May 2011 local time, a team of 40 CIA-led Navy SEALs completed an operation to kill Osama bin Laden in Abbottabad, Pakistan about 35 miles (56 km) from Islamabad, the country's capital. The Navy SEALs were part of the Naval Special Warfare Development Group, previously called "Team 6". President Barack Obama later confirmed the death of bin Laden. The unprecedented media coverage raised the public profile of the SEAL community, particularly the counter-terrorism specialists commonly known as SEAL Team 6.

18. Are Navy Seals part of USSOCOM?

  a. Yes.

  b. No.

  c. Only for special operations.

  d. No, they are part of the US Navy.

20. What separates Navy SEALs from other military units?

    a. Belonging to NSWC.

    b. Direct action and special reconnaissance operations.

    c. Working underwater.

    d. Working for other military units in the world.

Mathematics

1. A map uses a scale of 1:100,000. How much distance on the ground is 3 inches on the map if the scale is in inches?

    a. 13 inches

    b. 300,000 inches

    c. 30,000 inches

    d. 333.999 inches

2. Divide 9.60 by 3.2.

    a. 2.50

    b. 3

    c. 2.3

    d. 6.4

3. Subtract 456,890 from 465,890.

    a. 9,000

    b. 7,000

    c. 8,970

    d. 8,500

4. Estimate 46,227 + 101,032.

    a. 14,700

    b. 147,000

    c. 14,700,000

    d. 104,700

5. Find the square of 25/9

    a. 5/3

    b. 3/5

    c. 7 58/81

    d. 15/2

6. Which one of the following is less than a third?

    a. 84/231

    b. 6/35

    c. 3/22

    d. b and c

7. Which of the following numbers is the largest?

    a. 1

    b. $\sqrt{2}$

    c. 3/2

    d. 4/3

8. 15/16 x 8/9 =

    a. 5/6

    b. 16/37

    c. 2/11

    d. 5/7

9. Driver B drove his car 20 km/h faster than the driver A, and driver B travelled 480 km 2 hours before driver A. What was the speed of driver A?

    a. 70

    b. 80

    c. 60

    d. 90

10. If a train travels at 72 kilometers per hour, how far will it travel in 12 seconds?

    a. 200 meters

    b. 220 meters

    c. 240 meters

    d. 260 meters

11. Tony bought 15 dozen eggs for \$80. 16 eggs were broken during loading and unloading. He sold the remaining eggs for \$0.54 each. What is his percent profit?

    a. 11%

    b. 11.2%

    c. 11.5%

    d. 12%

12. In a class of 83 students, 72 are present. What percent of students are absent?

    a. 12%

    b. 13%

    c. 14%

    d. 15%

13. In a local election at polling station A, 945 voters cast their vote out of 1270 registered voters. At polling station B, 860 cast their vote out of 1050 registered voters and at station C, 1210 cast their vote out of 1440 registered voters. What was the total turnout including all three polling stations?

    a. 70%

    b. 74%

    c. 76%

    d. 80%

14. Estimate 5205 ÷ 25

    a. 108

    b. 308

    c. 208

    d. 408

15. 7/15 – 3/10 =

    a. 1/6

    b. 4/5

    c. 1/7

    d. 1 1/3

16. Susan wants to buy a leather jacket that costs $545.00 and is on sale for 10% off. What is the approximate cost?

    a. $525

    b. $450

    c. $475

    d. $500

17. 11/20 ÷ 9/20 =

    a. 99/20

    b. 4 19/20

    c. 1 2/9

    d. 1 1/9

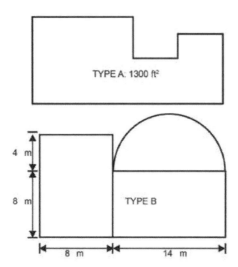

18. The price of houses in a certain subdivision is based on the total area. Susan is watching her budget and wants to choose the house with the lowest area. Which house type, A (1300 ft²) or B, should she choose if she would like the house with the lowest price? (1cm² = 4.0ft² & π = 22/7)

    a. Type B is smaller 140 ft²

    b. Type A is smaller

    c. Type B is smaller at 855 ft²

    d. Type B is larger

19. Estimate 2009 x 108.

   a. 110,000

   b. 2,0000

   c. 21,000

   d. 210,000

20. Simplify 0.12 + 1 2/5 – 1 3/5

   a. 1 1/25

   b. 1 3/25

   c. 1 2/5

   d. 2 3/5

Algebra

21. Using the quadratic formula, solve the quadratic equation: $0.9x^2 + 1.8x - 2.7 = 0$

   a. 1 and 3

   b. -3 and 1

   c. -3 and -1

   d. -1 and 3

22. Subtract polynomials $4x^3 - 2x^2 - 10$ and $5x^3 + x^2 + x + 5$.

   a. $-x^3 - 3x^2 - x - 15$

   b. $9x^3 - 3x^2 - x - 15$

   c. $-x^3 - x^2 + x - 5$

   d. $9x^3 - x^2 + x + 5$

23. Find x and y from the following system of equations:

(4x + 5y)/3 = ((x - 3y)/2) + 4
(3x + y)/2 = ((2x + 7y)/3) -1

    a. (1, 3)

    b. (2, 1)

    c. (1, 1)

    d. (0, 1)

24. Using the factoring method, solve the quadratic equation: $x^2 + 12x - 13 = 0$

    a. -13 and 1

    b. -13 and -1

    c. 1 and 13

    d. -1 and 13

25. Using the quadratic formula, solve the quadratic equation:

$$\frac{x+2}{x-2} + \frac{x-2}{x+2} = 0$$

    a. It has infinite numbers of solutions

    b. 0 and 1

    c. It has no solutions

    d. 0

26. Turn the following expression into a simple polynomial:

$5(3x^2 - 2) - x^2(2 - 3x)$

    a. $3x^3 + 17x^2 - 10$

    b. $3x^3 + 13x^2 + 10$

    c. $-3x^3 - 13x^2 - 10$

    d. $3x^3 + 13x^2 - 10$

27. Solve $(x^3 + 2)(x^2 - x) - x^5$.

    a. $2x^5 - x^4 + 2x^2 - 2x$

    b. $-x^4 + 2x^2 - 2x$

    c. $-x^4 - 2x^2 - 2x$

    d. $-x^4 + 2x^2 + 2x$

28. $9ab^2 + 8ab^2 =$

    a. ab^2

    b. $17ab^2$

    c. 17

    d. $17a^2b^2$

29. Factor the polynomial $x^2 - 7x - 30$.

    a. $(x + 15)(x - 2)$

    b. $(x + 10)(x - 3)$

    c. $(x - 10)(x + 3)$

    d. $(x - 15)(x + 2)$

30. If a and b are real numbers, solve the following equation: $(a + 2)x - b = -2 + (a + b)x$

    a. -1

    b. 0

    c. 1

    d. 2

31. If $A = -2x^4 + x^2 - 3x$, $B = x^4 - x^3 + 5$ and $C = x^4 + 2x^3 + 4x + 5$, find $A + B - C$.

    a. $x^3 + x^2 + x + 10$

    b. $-3x^3 + x^2 - 7x + 10$

    c. $-2x^4 - 3x^3 + x^2 - 7x$

    d. $-3x^4 + x^3 + x^2 - 7x$

32. $(4Y^3 - 2Y^2) + (7Y^2 + 3y - y) =$

    a. $4y^3 + 9y^2 + 4y$

    b. $5y^3 + 5y^2 + 3y$

    c. $4y^3 + 7y^2 + 2y$

    d. $4y^3 + 5y^2 + 2y$

33. Turn the following expression into a simple polynomial: $1 - x(1 - x(1 - x))$

    a. $x^3 + x^2 - x + 1$

    b. $-x^3 - x^2 + x + 1$

    c. $-x^3 + x^2 - x + 1$

    d. $x^3 + x^2 - x - 1$

34. $7(2y + 8) + 1 - 4(y + 5) =$

    a. $10y + 36$

    b. $10y + 77$

    c. $18y + 37$

    d. $10y + 37$

35. Richard gives 's' amount of salary to each of his 'n' employees weekly. If he has 'x' amount of money then how many days he can employ these 'n' employees.

    a. $sx/7n$

    b. $7x/nx$

    c. $nx/7s$

    d. $7x/ns$

36. Factor the polynomial $x^2 - 3x - 4$.

    a. $(x + 1)(x - 4)$

    b. $(x - 1)(x + 4)$

    c. $(x - 1)(x - 4)$

    d. $(x + 1)(x + 4)$

37. Solve the inequality:

2x + 1/2x - 1 < 1

    a. $(-2, +\infty)$
    b. $(1, +\infty)$
    c. $(-\infty, -2)$
    d. $(-\infty, 1/2)$

38. Using the quadratic formula, solve the quadratic equation:

$(a^2 - b^2)x^2 + 2ax + 1 = 0$

    a. $a/(a + b)$ and $b/(a + b)$
    b. $1/(a + b)$ and $a/(a + b)$
    c. $a/(a + b)$ and $a/(a - b)$
    d. $-1/(a + b)$ and $1/(a - b)$

39. Turn the following expression into a simple polynomial: **(a + b) (x + y) + (a - b) (x - y) - (ax + by)**

    a. $ax + by$
    b. $ax - by$
    c. $ax^2 + by^2$
    d. $ax^2 - by^2$

40. Given polynomials A = $4x^5 - 2x^2 + 3x - 2$ and B = $-3x^4 - 5x^2 - 4x + 5$, find A + B.

    a. $x^5 - 3x^2 - x - 3$
    b. $4x^5 - 3x^4 + 7x^2 + x + 3$
    c. $4x^5 - 3x^4 - 7x^2 - x + 3$
    d. $4x^5 - 3x^4 - 7x^2 - x - 7$

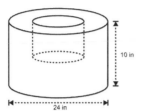

41. What is the volume of the above solid made by a hollow cylinder with half in size of the larger cylinder?

    a. 1440 π in³

    b. 1260 π in³

    c. 1040 π in³

    d. 960 π in³

42. Find x if $\log_{1/2} x = 4$.

    a. 16

    b. 8

    c. 1/8

    d. 1/16

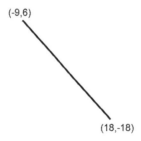

43. What is the slope of the line above?

    a. -8/9

    b. 9/8

    c. -9/8

    d. 8/9

44. If the sequence {a$_n$} is defined by a$_{n+1}$ = 1- a$_n$ and a$_2$ = 6, find a$_4$.

    a. 2

    b. 1

    c. 6

    d. -1

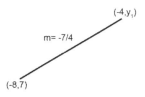

45. With the data given above, what is the value of y$_1$?

    a. 0

    b. -7

    c. 7

    d. 8

46. The area of a rectangle is 20 cm². If one side increases by 1 cm and other by 2 cm, the area of the new rectangle is 35 cm². Find the sides of the original rectangle.

    a. (4,8)

    b. (4,5)

    c. (2.5,8)

    d. b and c

47. Solve log$_{10}$10,000 = x.

    a. 2

    b. 4

    c. 3

    d. 6

(18,12)

(9,-6)

48. What is the distance between the two points?

    a. ≈19

    b. 20

    c. ≈21

    d. ≈20

49. If in the right triangle, a is 12 and sinα=12/13, find cosα.

    a. -5/13

    b. -1/13

    c. 1/13

    d. 5/13

50. Find the solution for the following linear equation: 1/4 x - 2 = 5/6

    a. 0.2

    b. 0.4

    c. 0.6

    d. 0.8

(-1,2)

(-4,-4)

51. What is the slope of the line above?

    a. 1

    b. 2

    c. 3

    d. -2

52. How much water can be stored in a cylindrical container 5 meters in diameter and 12 meters high?

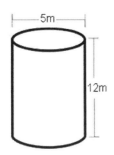

    a. 235.65 m^3

    b. 223.65 m^3

    c. 240.65 m^3

    d. 252.65 m^3

53. If members of the sequence {an} are represented by
$a_{n+1} = - a_{n-1}$ **and** $a_2 = 3$ **and, find** $a_3 + a_4$.

    a. 2

    b. 3

    c. 0

    d. -2

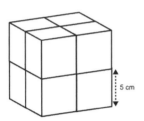

5 cm

54. What is the volume of the figure above?

    a. 125 cm³

    b. 875 cm³

    c. 1000 cm³

    d. 500 cm³

55. Solve

$x \sqrt{5} - y = \sqrt{5}$
$x - y \sqrt{5} = 5$

    a. $(0, -\sqrt{5})$

    b. $(0, \sqrt{5})$

    c. $(-\sqrt{5}, 0)$

    d. $(\sqrt{5}, 0)$

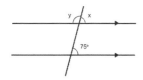

56. What is the value of the angle y?

    a. 25°

    b. 15°

    c. 30°

    d. 105°

57. Using the right triangle's legs, calculate (sinα + cosβ)/(tgα + ctgβ).

    a. a/b

    b. b/c

    c. b/a

    d. a/c

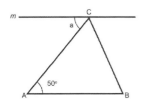

58. If the line m is parallel to the side AB of ΔABC, what is angle a?

    a. 130°

    b. 25°

    c. 65°

    d. 50°

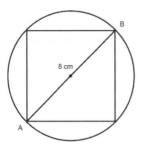

59. What is area of the circle?

    a. 4π cm²

    b. 12π cm²

    c. 10π cm²

    d. 16π cm²

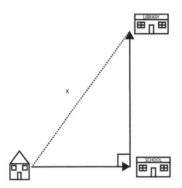

60. Every day starting from his home, Peter travels due east to school. After school, he travels due north to the library. This way Peter travels 25 kilometers. What is the distance between Peter's home and the library?

    a. 15 km

    b. 10 km

    c. 5 km

    d. 12 ½ km

Writing Skills

Directions: Select the best version of the underlined portion of the sentence

1. <u>Who</u> won first place in the Western Division?

   a. Whom won first place in the Western Division?

   b. Which won first place in the Western Division?

   c. What won first place in the Western Division?

   d. No change is necessary?

2. There are now several ways to listen to music, including radio, CDs, and Mp3 files <u>which</u> you can download onto an MP3 player.

   a. There are now several ways to listen to music, including radio, CDs, and Mp3 files on which you can download onto an MP3 player.

   b. There are now several ways to listen to music, including radio, CDs, and Mp3 files who you can download onto an MP3 player.

   c. There are now several ways to listen to music, including radio, CDs, and Mp3 files whom you can download onto an MP3 player.

   d. No change is necessary.

3. As the tallest monument in the United States, the St. Louis Arch <u>was rose to an impressive 630 feet</u>.

   a. As the tallest monument in the United States, the St. Louis Arch has rose to an impressive 630 feet.

   b. As the tallest monument in the United States, the St. Louis Arch is risen to an impressive 630 feet.

   c. As the tallest monument in the United States, the St. Louis Arch rises to an impressive 630 feet.

   d. No change is necessary.

4. The tired, old woman should <u>lain</u> on the sofa.

    a. The tired, old woman should lie on the sofa.

    b. The tired, old woman should lays on the sofa.

    c. The tired, old woman should laid on the sofa.

    d. No changes are necessary.

5. Did the students understand that Thanksgiving always <u>fallen</u> on the fourth Thursday in November?

    a No change is necessary.

    b. Did the students understand that Thanksgiving always falling on the fourth Thursday in November.

    c. Did the students understand that Thanksgiving always has fell on the fourth Thursday in November.

    d. Did the students understand that Thanksgiving always falls on the fourth Thursday in November.

6. Collecting stamps, <u>build models</u>, and listening to shortwave radio were Rick's main hobbies.

    a. Collecting stamps, building models, and listening to shortwave radio were Rick's main hobbies.

    b. Collecting stamps, to build models, and listening to shortwave radio were Rick's main hobbies.

    c. Collecting stamps, having built models, and listening to shortwave radio were Rick's main hobbies.

    d. No change is necessary.

7. This morning, <u>after the kids will leave for school</u> and before the sun came up, my mother makes herself a cup of cocoa.

a. This morning, after the kids had left for school and before the sun came up, my mother makes herself a cup of cocoa.

b. This morning, after the kids leave for school and before the sun came up, my mother makes herself a cup of cocoa.

c. This morning, after the kids have left for school and before the sun came up, my mother makes herself a cup of cocoa.

d. No change is necessary.

8. Elaine promised to bring the camera <u>to me</u> at the mall yesterday.

a. Elaine promised to bring the camera by me at the mall yesterday.

b. Elaine promised to bring the camera with me at the mall yesterday.

c. Elaine promised to bring the camera at me at the mall yesterday.

d. No changes are necessary.

9. Last night, he <u>laid</u> the sleeping bag down beside my mattress.

a. Last night, he lay the sleeping bag down beside my mattress.

b. Last night, he lain

c. Last night, he has laid

d. No change is necessary.

10. I would have bought the shirt for you <u>if I know</u> you liked it.

a. I would have bought the shirt for you if I had known you liked it.

b. I would have bought the shirt for you if I have known you liked it.

c. I would have bought the shirt for you if I would know you liked it.

d. No change is necessary.

11. George wrecked John's <u>car; that</u> was the end of their friendship.

a. George wrecked John's car that was the end of their friendship.

b. George wrecked John's car. that was the end of their friendship.

c. The sentence is correct.

d. None of the choices are correct.

12. The dress was not Gina's <u>favorite, however,</u> she wore it to the dance.

a. The dress was not Gina's favorite; however, she wore it to the dance.

b. None of the choices are correct.

c. The dress was not Gina's favorite, however; she wore it to the dance.

d. The dress was not Gina's favorite however, she wore it to the dance.

13. Chris showed his dedication to golf in many <u>ways;</u> <u>for</u> example, he watched all of the tournaments on television.

a. Chris showed his dedication to golf in many ways, for example, he watched all of the tournaments on television.

b. The sentence is correct.

c. Chris showed his dedication to golf in many ways, for example; he watched all of the tournaments on television.

d. Chris showed his dedication to golf in many ways for example he watched all of the tournaments on television.

14. Choose the sentence with the correct grammar.

a. If Joe had told me the truth, I wouldn't have been so angry.
b. If Joe would have told me the truth, I wouldn't have been so angry.
c. I wouldn't have been so angry if Joe would have told the truth.
d. If Joe would have telled me the truth, I wouldn't have been so angry.

15. Until you <u>take</u> the overdue books to the library, you can't <u>take</u> any new ones home.

a. Until you take the overdue books to the library, you can't take any new ones home
b. Until you take the overdue books to the library, you can't bring any new ones home.
c. Until you bring the overdue books to the library, you can't take any new ones home.
d. None of the choices are correct.

16. If they had <u>gone</u> to the party, he would have <u>gone</u> too.

    a. The sentence is correct.

    b. If they had went to the party, he would have gone too.

    c. If they had gone to the party, he would have went too.

    d. If they had went to the party, he would have went too.

17. His doctor suggested that he eat <u>fewer</u> snacks and do <u>fewer</u> lounging on the couch.

    a. His doctor suggested that he eat less snacks and do fewer lounging on the couch.

    b. His doctor suggested that he eat fewer snacks and do less lounging on the couch.

    c. His doctor suggested that he eat less snacks and do less lounging on the couch.

    d. None of the choices are correct.

18. I can never remember how to use those two common words, "sell," meaning to trade a product for money, or <u>"to sale,"</u> meaning an event where products are traded for less money than usual.

    a. sale-

    b. "sale,"

    c. "sale

    d. None of the above are correct.

19. His father is <u>poet and novelist.</u>

    a. a poet and novelist

    b. a poet and a novelist

    c. either of the above

    d. none of the above

20. The class just finished reading , <u>Leinengen versus the Ants</u> a short story by Carl Stephenson about a plantation owner's battle with army ants.

    a. -"Leinengen versus the Ants",

    b. Leinengen versus the Ants,

    c. "Leinengen versus the Ants,"

    d. None of the above

21. My best friend said, "<u>Always Count your Change</u>."

    a. My best friend said, "always count your change."

    b. The sentence is correct.

    c. My best friend said, "Always count your change."

    d. None of the choices are correct.

22. He told him to <u>raised</u> it up.

    a. He told him to rise it up

    b. He told him to raise it up

    c. Either of the above

    d. None of the above

23. I shall arrive early and <u>have</u> breakfast with you.

    a. I shall arrive early and I will have breakfast with you

    b. I shall arrive early and I would have breakfast with you

    c. The sentence is correct.

    d. None of the above

24. The gold coins with the diamonds <u>are</u> to be seized.

    a. The gold coins with the diamonds is to be seized

    b. The sentence is correct.

    c. None of the above

25. The trousers <u>is</u> to be delivered today.

    a The trousers are to be delivered today

    b. The sentence is correct

    c. Both of the above

26. She was nodding her head, her hips <u>were</u> swaying.

    a. She was nodding her head, her hips are swaying.

    b. She was nodding her head, her hips is swaying.

    c. The sentence is correct.

    d. None of the above

27. The sad news <u>are</u> delivered this morning.

    a. The sad news were delivered this morning

    b. The sentence is correct.

    c. The sad news was delivered this morning

    d. None of the above

28. <u>Mathematics were</u> my best subject in school.

    a. The sentence is correct

    b. Mathematics are my best subject in school

    c. Mathematics was my best subject in school

    d. None of the above

29. 15 minutes <u>is</u> all the time you have to complete the test.

    a. The sentence is correct.

    b. 15 minutes are all the time you have to complete the test.

    c. Both of the above.

    d. None of the above.

30. Everyone <u>have</u> to wear a black tie.

    a. Everyone are to wear a black tie.

    b. The sentence is correct.

    c. Everyone has to wear a black tie.

    d. None of the above.

Answer Key

Reading Comprehension

1. B
We can infer an important part of the respiratory system
are the lungs. From the passage, "Molecules of oxygen and
carbon dioxide are passively exchanged, by diffusion, between the gaseous external environment and the blood. This
exchange process occurs in the alveolar region of the lungs."
Therefore, one of the primary functions for the respiratory
system is the exchange of oxygen and carbon dioxide, and
this process occurs in the lungs. We can therefore infer that
the lungs are an important part of the respiratory system.

2. C
The process by which molecules of oxygen and carbon dioxide are passively exchanged is diffusion.
This is a definition type question. Scan the passage for references to "oxygen," "carbon dioxide," or "exchanged."

3. A
The organ that plays an important role in gas exchange in
amphibians is the skin.
Scan the passage for references to "amphibians," and find
the answer.

4. A
The three physiological zones of the respiratory system are
Conducting, transitional, respiratory zones.

5. A
We can infer that, an electrical discharge in the clouds
causes lightning.

The passage tells us that, "Lightning occurs when static
electricity inside clouds builds up and causes an electrical
charge,"

6. C
Being struck by lightning means, a ninety percent chance of

surviving the strike.

From the passage, "statistics show that 90% of victims survive a lightning blast."

7. A
We know that lightning is static electricity from the third sentence in the passage. We also know that water droplets colliding with ice crystals cause static electricity. Therefore, Lightning is caused by water droplets colliding with ice crystals.

8. A
Low blood sugar occurs both in diabetics and healthy adults.

9. B
None of the statements are the author's opinion.

10. A
The author's purpose is the inform.

11. A
The only statement that is not a detail is, "A doctor can diagnosis this medical condition by asking the patient questions and testing."

12. B
This passage describes the different categories for traditional stories. The other options are facts from the passage, not the main idea of the passage. The main idea of a passage will always be the most general statement. For example, Option A, Myths, fables, and folktales are not the same thing, and each describes a specific type of story. This is a true statement from the passage, but not the main idea of the passage, since the passage also talks about how some cultures may classify a story as a myth and others as a folktale. The statement, from Option B, Traditional stories can be categorized in different ways by different people, is a more general statement that describes the passage.

13. B
Option B is the best choice, categories that group traditional stories according to certain characteristics.

Options A and C are false and can be eliminated right away. Option D is designed to confuse. Option D may be true, but it is not mentioned in the passage.

14. D
The best answer is D, traditional stories themselves are a part of the larger category of folklore, which may also include costumes, gestures, and music.

All of the other options are false. Traditional stories are part of the larger category of Folklore, which includes other things, not the other way around.

15. A
The sentence is a recommendation.

16. C
Tips for a good night's sleep is the best alternative title for this article.

17. B
Mental activity is helpful for a good night's sleep is can not be inferred from this article.

18. C
This question tests the reader's vocabulary and contextualization skills. A may or may not be true, but focuses on the wrong function of the word "give" and ignores the rest of the sentence, which is more relevant to what the passage is discussing. B and D may also be selected if the reader depends too literally on the word "give", failing to grasp the more abstract function of the word that is the focus of answer C, which also properly acknowledges the entirety of the passage and its meaning.

19. A
Navy Seals are the maritime component of the United States Special Operations Command (USSOCOM).

20. C
Working underwater separates SEALs from other military units. This is taken directly from the passage.

Mathematics

1. B

1 inch on map = 100,000 inches on ground. So 3 inches on map = 3 x 100,000 = 300,000 inches on ground.

2. B

9.60/3.2 = 3

3. A

465,890 - 456,890 = 9,000.

4. B

46,227 + 101,032 is approximately 147,000. The exact answer is 147,259.

5. C

$(25/9)^2 = 625/81$

6. D

84/231 = 12/33 > 1/3
6/35 = 1/5 < 1/3
3/22 = 1/7 < 1/3

7. B

$\sqrt{2}$ is the largest number.
Here are the choices:

      a. 1

      b. $\sqrt{2}$ = 1.414

      c. 3/22 = .1563

      d. 4/3 = 1.33

8. A

First cancel out 15/16 x 8/9 to get 5/2 x 1/3, then multiply numerators and denominators to get 5/6.

9. B

$V_b = V_a - 20$
$S = 480$
$t_a + 2 = t_b$

$S = V_a t_a$

$t_a = S/V_a$

$S = V_b t_b$

$480 = (V_a - 20)(t_a + 2)$

$480 = (V_a - 20)(480/V_a + 2)$

$480 = 480 + 2V_a - 2 - 480/V_a - 40$

$2V_a^2 - 40V_a - 9600 = 0$

$V_a^2 - 20V_a - 4800 = 0$

$V_{a1,2} = 20 \pm \sqrt{400 + 4 - 4800} / 2$

$V_{a1,2} = 20 \pm 140 / 2$

$V_a = 80$

10. C
1 hour is equal to 3600 seconds and 1 kilometer is equal to 1000 meters. So a train covers 72,000 meters in 36,000 seconds.
Distance covered in 12 seconds = 12 × 72,000/3,600 = 240 meters.

11. A
Remaining number of eggs that Tony sold = (12 × 15) − 16 = 164. Total amount for selling 164 eggs = 164×0.54 = $88.56.
Percentage profit = (88.56 − 80) × 100/80 = 10.7%
The answer is required with 2 significant digits, round off to 11%.

12. B
Absent students = 83 − 72 = 11
Percent of absent students = 11/83 X 100 = 13.25
Reducing up to two significant digits = 13%.

13. D
Total votes cast = 945 + 860 + 1210 = 3015
Total registered voters at all 3 polling stations =
1270 + 1050 + 1440 = 3760
Turnout = 3015/3760 X 100 = 80%

14. C
The approximate answer to 5205 ÷ 25 is 208. The exact answer is 208.2.

15. A
A common denominator is needed, a number which both 15 and 10 will divide into. So 14-9/30 = 5/30 = 1/6

16. D
The jacket costs $545.00 so we can round up to $550. 10% of $550 is 55. We can round down to $50, which is easier to work with. $550 - $50 is $500. The jacket will cost about $500.

The actual cost is 545-54.50 = 490.50.

17. C
11/20 x 20/9 = 11/1 x 1/9 = 11/9 = 1 2/9

18. C
Area of Type B = [(12 x 8) + (14 x 8) + (1/2 x 22/7 x 7^2)]
96 + 112 + 77
285 m^2
Converting to feet = 3 x 285 ft^2
Area of Type B = 855 ft^2

19. D
2009 x 108 is approximately 210,000. The exact answer is 216,972.

20. B
0.12 + 2/5 + 3/5, Convert decimal to fraction to get 3/25 + 2/5 + 3/5, = (3 + 10 + 15)/25, = 28/25 = 1 3/25

21. B
$0.9x^2$ + 1.8x - 2.7 = 0 * 10

$9x^2$ + 18x - 27 = 0 ÷ 9
x^2 + 2x - 3 = 0

$x_{1,2}$ = -2 $\pm$ $\sqrt{2^2}$ - 4 * (-3)/2
$x_{1,2}$ = -2 $\pm$ $\sqrt{4}$ + 12/2
$x_{1,2}$ = -2 $\pm$ $\sqrt{16}$/2
$x_{1,2}$ = -2 $\pm$ 4
x_1 = -2 + 4/2 = 1

$x_2 = -2 - 4/2 = -3$

22. A
$(4x^3 - 2x^2 - 10) - (5x^3 + x^2 + x + 5)$
$4x^3 - 2x^2 - 10 - 5x^3 - x^2 - x - 5$
$-x^3 - 3x^2 - x - 15$

23. C
Divide both equations by 6, for,

$2(4x + 5y) = 3(x - 3y) + 24$
$3(3x + 7) = 2(2x + 7y) - 6$

$8x + 10y = 3x - 9y + 24$
$9x + 3y = 4x + 14y = 6$

$8x + 10y = 3x - 9y + 24$
$9x + 3y = 4x + 14y - 6$

$5x + 19y = 24$
$5x = 11y = -6$

$5x + 19y - (5x - 11y) = 24 - (-6)$
$5x + 19y - 5x + 11y = 24 + 6$

$30y = 30$
y = 1

$5x + 19y = 24$

$5x + 19 = 24$

$5x = 24 - 19 = 5$

x = 1

24. A
-13 and 1
$x^2 + 12x - 13$
$x^2 + 13x - x - 13 = 0$
$x(x + 13) - (x + 13) = 0$
$(x + 13)(x - 1) = 0$
$X = -13 \quad X = 1$

25. C
This equation has no solution.

$x^2 + 4x + 4 + x^2 - 4x + 4 / (x - 2)(x + 2) = 0$

$2x^2 + 8 / (x - 2)(x + 2) = 0 => 2x^2 + 8 = 0$
$x^2 + 4 = 0$
$x_{1,2} = 0 \pm \sqrt{-4 * 4} / 2$
$x_{1,2} = 0 \pm \sqrt{-16} / 2$
Solution for the square root of -16 is not a real number, so this equation has no solution.

26. D
$3x^3 + 13x^2 - 10$
$5(3x^2 - 2) - x^2(2 - 3x)$
$15x^2 - 10 - 2x^2 + 3x^3$
$3x^3 + 13x^2 - 10$

27. B
$-x^4 + 2x^2 - 2x$
$(x^3 + 2)(x^2 - x) - x^5$
$x^5 - x^4 + 2x^2 - 2x - x^5$
$-x^4 + 2x^2 - 2x$

28. B
$ab^2 (9 + 8) = 17ab^2$

29. C
$x^2 - 7x - 30 = x * x - 10x + 3x - 3 * 10 = x(x - 10) + 3(x - 10) =$
$(x - 10)(x + 3)$

30. A
$(a + 2)x - b = -2 + (a + b)x$
$ax + 2x - b = -2 + ax + bx$
$ax + 2x - ax - bx = -2 + b$
$2x - bx = -2 + b$
$(2 - b)x = -(2 - b)$
$x = -(2 - b) : (2 - b)$
$x = -1$

31. C
$-2x^4 - 3x^3 + x^2 - 7x$
$A + B - C = (-2x^4 + x^2 - 3x) + (x^4 - x^3 + 5) - (x^4 + 2x^3 + 4x + 5)$
$-2x^4 + x^2 - 3x + x^4 - x^3 + 5 - x^4 - 2x^3 - 4x - 5$
$-2x^4 - 3x^3 + x^2 - 7x$

32. D
Remove parenthesis
$4Y^3 - 2Y^2 + 7Y^2 + 3Y - Y =$
add and subtract like terms, $4Y^3 + 5Y^2 + 2Y$

33. C
$1 - x(1 - x(1 - x))$
$1 - x(1 - x + x^2)$
$1 - x + x^2 - x^3$
$-x^3 + x^2 - x + 1$

34. D
Open parenthesis, $(7 \times 2y + 7 \times 8) + 1 - (4 \times y -20) =$
$14y + 56 + 1 - 4y - 20$,
Collect like terms $=14y -4y + 56 + 1 - 20 = 10y + 37$

35. D
He pays 'ns' amount to the employees for 7 days. The 'x' amount will be for '7x/ns' days.

36. A
$x^2 - 3x - 4 = x * x + x - 4x - 4 = x(x + 1) - 4(x + 1) = (x + 1)(x - 4)$

37. D
$(2x + 1 /2x - 1) < 1$
$(2x + 1 /2x - 1) - 1 < 0$
$(2x + 1 - 2x + 1/2x - 1) < 0$
$2/2x - 1 < 0$

2 is a positive number, so

$2x - 1 < 0$
$2x < 1$
$x < 1/2$

38. D

$$-\frac{1}{a+b} \text{ and } -\frac{1}{a-b}$$

$$(a^2-b^2)x^2+2ax+1=0$$

$$x_{1,2}=\frac{-2a\pm\sqrt{(2a)^2-4(a^2-b^2)}}{2(a^2-b^2)}$$

$$x_{1,2}=\frac{-2a\pm\sqrt{4a^2-4a^2+4b^2}}{2(a^2-b^2)}$$

$$x_{1,2}=\frac{-2a\pm\sqrt{4b^2}}{2(a^3-b^2)}$$

$$x_{1,2}=\frac{-2a\pm 2b}{2(a^2-b^3)}$$

$$x_{1,2}=\frac{-a\pm b}{a^2-b^2}=\frac{-a\pm b}{(a-b)(a+b)}$$

$$x_1=\frac{-a+b}{(a-b)(a+b)}=\frac{-(a-b)}{(a-b)(a+b)}=-\frac{1}{(a+b)}$$

$$x_2=\frac{-a-b}{(a-b)(a+b)}=\frac{-(a+b)}{(a-b)(a+b)}=-\frac{1}{(a-b)}$$

39. A

(a + b) (x + y) + (a - b) (x - y) - (ax + by)
= ax + ay + bx + by + ax - ay - bx + by - ax - by
ax + by

40. C

$4x^5 - 3x^4 - 7x^2 - x + 3$
A + B = $(4x^5 - 2x^2 + 3x - 2) + (-3x^4 - 5x^2 - 4x + 5)$=
$4x^5 - 2x^2 + 3x - 2 - 3x^4 - 5x^2 - 4x + 5$
$4x^5 - 3x^4 - 7x^2 - x + 3$

41. B

Total Volume = Volume of large cylinder - Volume of small cylinder
Volume of cylinder = area of base x height
Volume= (π 12^2x 10) - (π 6^2x 5), 1440π - 180π
Volume= 1260π in^3

42. D

$\log_{1/2}x = 4$
$(1/2)^4 = x$
x = 1/16

43. A

Slope (m) = $\dfrac{\text{change in y}}{\text{change in x}}$

$(x_1, y_1)=(-9,6)$ & $(x_2, y_2)= (18,-18)$
Slope = $(-18 - 6)/[18-(-9)]= -24/27 = -8/9$

44. C
$a_{n+1} = 1 - a_n$
$a_2 = 6$
$a_3 = 1- a_2 = 1 - 6 = -5$
$a_4 = 1 - a_3 = 1 - (-5) = 1 + 5 = 6$

45. A
$x_1, = -4$, $(x_2, y_2)= (-8,7)$ & slope = $-7/4$
$(7 - y_1)/[-8-(-4)]= -7/4$
$(7 - y_1)/-4= -7/4$
$7 - y_1 = 7$
$y_1 = 0$

46. D
$ab = 20 => a = 20/b$
$(a + 1) (b + 2) = 35$

$(20/b + 1) (b + 2) = 35$
$20 + 40/b + b + 2 = 35$
$20b + 40 + b^2 = 33b$
$b^2 - 13b + 40 = 0$
$b_{1,2} = 13 \pm \sqrt{169 - 160} / 2$
$b_{1,2} = 13 \pm 3 / 2$
$b_1 = 8$
$b_2 = 5$
$a_1 = 20/b_1 = 20/8 = 2.5$
$a_2 = 20/b_2 = 20/5 = 4$

47. B
$\log_{10} 10,000 = x$
$10^x = 10,000$
$10^x = 10^4$
$x = 4$

48. D
Distance between 2 points = $[(x_2 - x_1)^2+(y_2 - y_1)^2]^{1/2}$

Distance= $[(18 - 9)^2 + (12 + 6)^2]^{1/2}$
Distance= $[(9)^2 + (18)^2]^{1/2}$
Distance= $(81 + 324)^{1/2}$

Distance= $(405)^{1/2}$
Since $20^2 = 400$ & $21^2 = 441$, $19^2 = 361$ therefore the distance is approximately 20.

49. D

a = 12
$\sin a = 12/13 = a/c$
$a/c = 12/13$
$12/c = 12/13$
c = 13
$a^2 + b^2 = c^2$
$12^2 + b^2 = 13^2$
$b^2 = 169 - 144$
$b^2 = 25$
b = 5
$\cos a = b/c = 5/13$

50. D

1/4x - 2 = 5/6
$1 = 5 (4x - 2)/6$
$6 = 5(4x - 2)$
$6 = 20x - 10$
$-20x = -10 - -6$
$-20x = -16$
x = -16/-20 = 0.8

51. B

Slope (m) = <u>change in y</u>
             change in x

$(x_1, y_1) = (-1, 2)$ & $(x_2, y_2) = (-4, -4)$
Slope = $(-4 - 2)/[-4 - (-1)] = -6/-3$
Slope = 2

52. B

The formula of the volume of cylinder is = Π r^2h. Where Π is 3.142, r is radius of the cross sectional area, and h is the height. So the volume will be = $3.142 \times 2.5^2 \times 12 = 235.65$ m^3.

53. C

$a_{n+1} = - a_{n-1}$
$a_2 = 3$
$a_3 = - a_2 = -3$
$a_4 = - a_3 = -(-3) = 3$

$a_3 + a_4 = -3 + 3 = 0$

54. C
Large cube is made up of 8 smaller cubes of 5 cm sides.
Volume = Volume of small cube x 8
Volume = (5 x 5 x 5) x 8, 125 x 8
Volume = 1000 cm³

55. A
$(0, -\sqrt5)$

$y = x\sqrt5 - \sqrt5$
$x - (x\sqrt5 - \sqrt5) \sqrt5 = 5$
$x - 5x + 5 = 5$
$-4x = 5 - 5$
$-4x = 0$

$y = x\sqrt5 - \sqrt5$
$y = 0\sqrt5 - \sqrt5$
$y = \sqrt5$

Remove the brackets, but change all signs in the third poly-nomial because of the minus sign. Now group the variables by degrees.

56. D
Two parallel lines intersected by a third line with angles of 75°
x = 75° (corresponding angles)
x + y = 180° (supplementary angles)
y = 180° - 75°
y = 105°

57. B
$(\sin\alpha + \cos\beta)/(tg\alpha + ctg\beta) = (a/c + a/c)/(a/b + a/b) = (2a/c)/(2a/b) = b/c$

58. D
Two parallel lines(m & side AB) intersected by side AC
a = 50° (interior angles).

59. D
Circle with given diameter and a square within the circle

Area of circle = π x r²
Area of circle = π x 4²
Area of circle = 16 π cm²

The actual cost will be 10% X 545 = $54.50
545 – 54.50 = $490.50

60. C
Pythagorean Theorem:
(Hypotenuse)² = (Perpendicular)² + (Base)²
$h^2 = a^2 + b^2$

Given: $a^2 + b^2 = 25$
$h^2 = 25$
h = 5, so the distance from Peter's home to the library is 5 km.

Writing Skills

1. D
"Who" is correct because the question uses an active construction. "To whom was first place given?" is passive construction.

2. D
"Which" is correct, because the files are objects and not people.

3. C
The simple present tense, "rises," is correct.

4. A
"Lie" does not require a direct object, while "lay" does. The old woman might lie on the couch, which has no direct object, or she might lay the book down, which has the direct object, "the book."

5. D
The simple present tense, "falls," is correct because it is repeated action.

6. A
The present progressive, "building models," is correct in this sentence; it is required to match the other present progressive

verbs.

7. C
Past Perfect tense describes a completed action in the past, before another action in the past.

8. D
The preposition "to" is the correct preposition to use with "bring."

9. D
"Laid" is the past tense.

10. A
This is a past unreal conditional sentence. It requires an 'if' clause and a result clause, and either clause can appear first. The 'if' clause uses the past perfect, while the result clause uses the past participle.

11. C
The semicolon links independent clauses. An independent clause can form a complete sentence by itself.

12. A
The semicolon links independent clauses with a conjunction (However).

13. B
The sentence is correct. The semicolon links independent clauses. An independent clause can form a complete sentence by itself.

14. A
The third conditional is used for talking about an unreal situation (that did not happen) in the past. For example, "If I had studied harder, [if clause] I would have passed the exam [main clause]. Which is the same as, "I failed the exam, because I didn't study hard enough."

15. C
Bring vs. Take. Usage depends on your location. Something coming your way is brought to you. Something going away is taken from you.

16. A
The sentence is correct. Went vs. Gone. Went is the simple past tense. Gone is used in the past perfect.

17. B
Fewer vs. Less. 'Fewer' is used with countables and 'less' is used with uncountables.

18. B
Here the word "sale" is used as a "word" and not as a word in the sentence, so quotation marks are used.

19. B
His father is a poet and a novelist. It is necessary to use 'a' twice in this sentence for the two distinct things.

20. C
Titles of short stories are enclosed in quotation marks, and commas always go inside quotation marks.

21. A
Quoted speech is not capitalized.

22. B
The verb raise ('to increase', 'to lift up.') can appear in three forms, raise, raised and raised.

23. C
The two verbs "shall" and "will" should not be used in the same sentence when referring to the same future.

24. B
When two subjects are linked with "with" or "as well," use the verb form that matches the first subject.

25. A
Use a plural verb for nouns like measles, tongs, trousers, riches, scissors etc.

26. C
A verb can fit any of the two subjects in a compound sentence since the verb form agrees with that subject.

27. C
Always use the singular verb form for nouns like politics, wages, mathematics, innings, news, advice, summons, furniture, information, poetry, machinery, vacation, scenery etc.

28. C
Always use the singular verb form for nouns like politics, wages, mathematics, innings, news, advice, summons, furniture, information, poetry, machinery, vacation, scenery etc.

29. A
Use a singular verb with a plural noun that refers to a specific amount or quantity that is considered as a whole (dozen, hundred score etc).

30. C
Use a singular verb with either, each, neither, everyone and many.

Conclusion

CONGRATULATIONS! You have made it this far because you have applied yourself diligently to practicing for the exam and no doubt improved your potential score considerably! Getting into a good school is a huge step in a journey that might be challenging at times but will be many times more rewarding and fulfilling. That is why being prepared is so important.

Good Luck!

FREE Ebook Version

Download a FREE Ebook version of the publication!

Suitable for tablets, iPad, iPhone, or any smart phone.

Go to
http://www.tinyurl.com/ o3vd9k8

Register for Free Updates and More Practice Test Questions

Register your purchase at www.test-preparation.ca/register. html for fast and convenient access to updates, errata, free test tips and more practice test questions.

Learn to increase your score using time-tested secrets for answering multiple choice questions!

This practice book has everything you need to know about answering multiple choice questions on a standardized test!

You will learn 12 strategies for answering multiple choice questions and then practice each strategy with over 45 reading comprehension multiple choice questions, with extensive commentary from exam experts!

Maybe you have read this kind of thing before, and maybe feel you don't need it, and you are not sure if you are going to buy this Book.

Remember though, it only a few percentage points divide the PASS from the FAIL students.

Even if our multiple choice strategies increase your score by a few percentage points, isn't that worth it?

Get Organized, Study Less and Get Higher Marks!

Here is what you will learn:

- How to Organize your Study Space

- Four different strategies for taking notes

- Reading strategies for textbooks, essays, novels and literature

- How to Concentrate - What is concentration and how do you do it!

- Using Flash Cards - Complete guide to using flash cards including the Leitner method.

and LOT more... Including time management, sleep, nutrition, motivation, brain food, procrastination, study schedules and more!

Go to https://www.createspace.com/4060298

Enter Code LYFZGQB5 for 25% off!

Endnotes

Reading Comprehension passages where noted below are used under the Creative Commons Attribution-ShareAlike 3.0 License

http://en.wikipedia.org/wiki/Wikipedia:Text_of_Creative_Commons_Attribution-ShareAlike_3.0_Unported_License

[1] Immune System. In *Wikipedia*. Retrieved November 12, 2010 from, en.wikipedia.org/wiki/Immune_system.
[2] White Blood Cell. In *Wikipedia*. Retrieved November 12, 2010 from en.wikipedia.org/wiki/White_blood_cell.
[3] Infectious disease. In *Wikipedia*. Retrieved November 12, 2010 from http://en.wikipedia.org/wiki/Infectious_disease.
[4] Thunderstorm. In *Wikipedia*. Retrieved November 12, 2010 from en.wikipedia.org/wiki/Thunderstorm.
[5] Meteorology. In *Wikipedia*. Retrieved November 12, 2010 from en.wikipedia.org/wiki/Outline_of_meteorology.
[6] Cloud. In *Wikipedia*. Retrieved November 12, 2010 from http://en.wikipedia.org/wiki/Clouds.
[7] U.S. Navy Seal. In *Wikipedia*. Retrieved November 12, 2010 from en.wikipedia.org/wiki/United_States_Navy_SEALs.
[8] Respiratory System. In *Wikipedia*. Retrieved November 12, 2010 from en.wikipedia.org/wiki/Respiratory_system.
[9] Mythology. In *Wikipedia*. Retrieved November 12, 2010 from en.wikipedia.org/wiki/Mythology.